WORSHIP
LIKE
JESUS

CONSTANCE M. CHERRY

WORSHIP LIKE JESUS

A Guide for Every Follower

Abingdon Press

Nashville

WORSHIP LIKE JESUS:
A GUIDE FOR EVERY FOLLOWER

Copyright © 2019 by Constance M. Cherry

Library of Congress Cataloging-in-Publication Data has been requested.

ISBN 978-1-5018-8147-3

19 20 21 22 23 24 25 26 27 28 29—10 9 8 7 6 5 4 3 2 1
MANUFACTURED IN THE UNITED STATES OF AMERICA

In loving memory of

Betty L. Stiles (1940–2018)
and
John D. Stiles (1934–2018),

true disciples, true worshipers, true friends

CONTENTS

ACKNOWLEDGMENTS

No one undertakes a major endeavor such as the writing of this book without the support of many people. To each one of the persons who participated in some way in the production of this manuscript, I am most grateful.

Foremost in my mind is the Prayer Circle of people who committed to praying for me throughout the many months of the project. You know who you are. I have keenly felt your support. I am also aware of many individuals who have lifted me in prayer voluntarily, chief among them my dad, the Reverend Dr. Harold R. Cherry, who at age ninety-three continues his life of disciplined intercessory prayer for many people.

I am thankful for the congregation of Grant United Methodist Church (Fairmount, Indiana) that I serve as pastor. They will never know how much their love and support mean to me. They think I minister to them, but I believe it is the other way around. They encourage me in all of my endeavors by generously making it possible for me to fulfill God's call widely. The mutual affection we experience is a gift from God.

I thank my remarkable students in the worship programs at Indiana Wesleyan University for their prayers, interest in my work, and, yes, friendship. Their sincere dedication to Christ and his church is inspiring to me. They teach me so much and give me great joy on a daily basis. I can't help but write with their faces before me.

I express sincere thanks to Indiana Wesleyan University for its support through granting me the University Scholar Award, which afforded classroom release time to assist me in the writing of this book.

Acknowledgments

Great appreciation goes to Jessica Dion for her excellent work in editing the manuscript, sense of professionalism, and positive spirit.

Special thanks to Benjamin Snoek—a leader among the worship majors at Indiana Wesleyan University and promising worship architect—for designing the artistic graphics included throughout the book.

I am grateful for the support of Senior Acquisitions Editor Constance Stella and to Abingdon Press for welcoming my small contribution to its collection of resources for the church.

Last, the influence of my mentor and friend Robert E. Webber (1933–2007) is forever stamped upon my heart, mind, and ministry, though he left us long ago. His voice can now be heard among those in the glorified community where the worship he spoke of with such passion and anticipation as my teacher has become his reality. He used to worship like Jesus. Today he worships with Jesus. Thanks be to God!

THE CALL TO WORSHIP

Worship in local churches has changed dramatically over the past fifty years, not just in North America. We are left with some questions:

- Have these widespread and varying shifts resulted in a vague or even false impression of what the weekly worship event is all about?
- Do followers of Jesus Christ grasp the importance of their role in worship?
- Do they know how to become fully engaged participants?
- Do they realize Jesus himself is our best guide and model for worship?

This book is not about worship wars, which style is best, or the latest trends. It is about more important things. This book is for followers of Jesus who long to become more engaged worshipers. It is a guide for laypersons who may have never been taught how to worship God. In a nutshell, this book is about worship discipleship. Discipleship is the journey of being transformed into the likeness of Jesus Christ. Many plans have approached discipleship topically by training believers how to pray, how to read the Bible, how to share their faith, how to serve others, and so on. As necessary as these things are, what is typically omitted is the most important training of all: how to worship God.

Worshiping the triune God in community is the most significant ongoing ministry of the local church. Worship is the heartbeat of the relationship between God and believers; consequently, it is also the dynamic force that undergirds all of the church's ministries as she seeks to faithfully live into the kingdom of God. Yet decades of worship experimentation in response to dramatic cultural shifts have left many Christians with misconceptions. Now more than ever, worship discipleship is needed.

Worship Like Jesus guides Christ-followers through the essential features of Christian worship, transforming the reader's understanding and experience of worship, leading people—even entire congregations—to experience worship in exciting and profound ways as never before, resulting in deeper and more committed discipleship. It does so by exploring how Jesus goes before us as a worshiper to show us the way.

This book promises to open up new vistas for the individual reader; however, it is best read with other Christians who are seeking greater understanding about worship, for discipleship happens most effectively in community. It is written with groups of believers in mind and is therefore well suited for use by small groups, Sunday school classes, Bible study groups, worship teams, church staffs, weekend retreats, and book study groups—in short, wherever two or three are gathered.

As a way of enabling spiritual formation, each chapter of *Worship Like Jesus* follows the same helpful pattern:

- describing how we worship now
- discovering how Jesus worshiped
- deliberating how Jesus would worship today
- determining how we will worship as Jesus's disciples

In addition, current challenges are addressed and reflection questions are provided at the end of each chapter, along with a concluding prayer.

Worship Like Jesus holds the potential to make a real difference in the life of each Christ-follower and their worshiping community. Imagine being surrounded by fully engaged, deeply committed disciples worshiping like Jesus! Your church may never be the same.

Worship is the regular, ongoing meeting

of a local body of Christian disciples with the triune God,

expressed in acts of corporate devotion done
in partnership with one another,

in order to give glory to God,

bear witness to their identity as God's people,

proclaim and celebrate the grand narrative
of God's eternal activity,

and receive power for living according
to God's kingdom purposes.

Constance M. Cherry

Chapter 1

OUR ROLE MODEL FOR WORSHIP

KEY QUESTION:
HOW DID JESUS WORSHIP?

A re you a leader or a follower? Chances are you've been asked that question at some point in time. Maybe it was an employer attempting to take you to the next level in the company, a school guidance counselor helping you decide on a career path, or a parent who was trying to get you on track after you started following the wrong crowd. Most of the time the role of leader is implied to be the better of the two options. Our culture tends to exalt leaders over followers.

By contrast, Jesus seems to view things a little differently. He presents an alternative picture of the measure of one's value. Unlike our bent toward exalting leadership, Jesus lifts up the role of follower—his follower. Jesus never issued a call to "Come lead with me," but he issued plenty of calls to "Come, follow me." (See Mark 1:17, 20; Matt 8:22, 9:9, etc.) Along the way, excellent followers become effective leaders, but they become special kinds of leaders— servant leaders—the kinds of leaders that God has in mind for the church and the world.

Describing How We Worship Now

Becoming a Disciple

Jesus used a very common word for those who would answer the call to follow him: *disciple*. A disciple is simply someone who devotedly follows a noted leader or teacher. Throughout time, many different religions, movements, or schools of thought have developed around a significant teacher who attracted learners who became disciples of their leader. The term is not unique to Christianity. In Jesus's own time there were many philosophers and rabbis who influenced a particular followership. Like them, Jesus consistently referred to his followers as his disciples. All Christians, by virtue of their allegiance to Jesus Christ, are known as his disciples.

A disciple is a learner. One who disciples others is a teacher. Discipleship is the process of becoming more and more like the teacher in one's thinking, practices, and way of life. By doing this, an end result is realized: the learner resembles the teacher. Teachers have the ultimate goal of reproducing themselves in their students; for example, a recognized artist who instructs her pupils in special techniques that influence their own budding artistic creations, or a social activist who pursues peace through nonviolence and helps others to do the same, or an athletic coach who imparts his particular method of performance on the field, and so forth. Good teachers not only instruct by using words. Perhaps more importantly, they influence their disciples through modeling their methods.

In the same way, every disciple has the ultimate goal of becoming like his or her teacher. The relationship between the teacher and the disciple is a close one. Disciples are serious about their followership. They watch the master teacher, listen, and ask questions, all the while noting the processes she or he uses to produce the end result. Disciples also use the same disciplines that are central to the teacher's approach. (Notice how closely the two words relate: disciples and

2

disciplines.) Particular disciplines help in the training process of becoming disciples who resemble the teacher.

Imitation is the key to discipleship. Step by step, through careful imitation, disciples become formed in the image of their teacher. Other people begin to identify disciples according to their resemblance to the teacher. As followers of Jesus, we spend significant time with the Master Teacher, discovering what is important to him, listening, questioning, processing, and observing, and all the while being formed in his image. As Jesus said, "Disciples aren't greater than their teacher, but whoever is fully prepared will be like their teacher" (Luke 6:40).

A New Take on WWJD

Quite a few years ago, an acronym became popular among some Christian groups. It appeared on wristbands, necklaces, bumper stickers, and posters. WWJD: What would Jesus do? The idea was that Christians should consider what Jesus would likely do in any given circumstance and then try to imitate him in their response. It was clever and no doubt helpful, but some folks had their questions. Could we positively know what Jesus would do in every situation? Is it possible to do the right actions without having the right heart? Should we focus on doing or being? Questions aside, the movement was well intentioned. WWJD bracelets are still around.

This book focuses on a different acronym: HWJW: How would Jesus worship? Have you ever thought about Jesus as a worshiper? How *did* Jesus worship? What were his patterns and priorities? What does he teach us through his actions related to worship? If we had only Jesus's life of worship to observe, what would we gain in our own worship discipleship?

If we had only Jesus's life of worship to observe, what would we gain in our own worship discipleship?

Here we have more concrete things to go on than mere speculation. We're not really left wondering what Jesus would do in worship; we can *see* what he did by reading the Gospel accounts of his life of worship while he was among us as a worshiper. And while it's possible to follow Jesus's worship patterns and do so without complete understanding at first, worship will form us as we continue in its discipline.

If our goal is to follow Jesus as his disciples in worship, we must ask this most important question: How did Jesus worship?

Key Question: How did Jesus worship?

Discovering How Jesus Worshiped

Worshiping Like Jesus: Discovering What Jesus Did and Taught

Jesus was a worshiper. And if discipleship is a matter of following the model and teachings of the Master, the starting place is to discover what the Master modeled and taught. We must understand the role worship played in his life so that we can follow his lead. He is our role model and mentor for discovering and practicing the essential aspects of worship as he lived them every day. It is incredibly important to examine Jesus's own life of worship so that we may answer these questions:

- What did Jesus do as a worshiper?
- What did Jesus teach about worship?
- What may we conclude was important to Jesus as a worshiper?
- What are the implications for Jesus's followers today as they worship?

4

What Jesus *did* and what he *taught* concerning worship are essential to know as Christ-followers. For how can we worship in ways that are pleasing to God unless we follow our Teacher in his ways of worship?

What did Jesus *do* as a worshiper? The four Gospel accounts of Jesus's life (Matthew, Mark, Luke, and John) present Jesus as someone who modeled a devoted and disciplined life of worship in community. He was a worshiper from birth who consistently, even daily, worshiped at the temple and the synagogue, kept the Sabbath, spent much time in prayer, participated in the regular worship rituals, worshiped God in defiance of Satan, read the scriptures in the synagogue service, cleansed the temple, celebrated the Jewish annual festivals of worship, pronounced blessings upon people, sang the liturgy, preached, and taught in the temple and synagogue. It is truly amazing to discover what was significant to Jesus when it came to public worship.

What did Jesus *teach* about worship? Again, with the Gospels as our source, we discover that Jesus provided oral instruction to his disciples. In so doing, he often challenged the status quo. He taught that the Father seeks worshipers, that worship is offered in spirit and in truth, that he was Lord even of the Sabbath, that there is an important connection between the sacrifices one presents to God and the kind of life one lives, that reconciliation has a lot to do with worship that is pleasing to God, that there are certain rules for public prayer, that sacrificial giving is pleasing to God, and that justice and mercy are the fruits of true worship. The Rabbi had some things to say about worship! Throughout the chapters of this book, these fascinating aspects of Jesus the worshiper will be explored in detail.

We have before us an urgent call to discover what our Teacher, Jesus, would show us if he were among us today. If we could watch him or hear him, what would we learn about worship? I imagine it might turn a few things upside down. Worship, as we have come to know it today, may even come unhinged. That's OK. Maybe it needs to. This book is about the importance of becoming Christian disciples who learn to worship God, and the best way to do so is by imitating Jesus's ways of worship. There's a lot to imitate, really, for there is more recorded in the Gospels about Jesus participating in worship than his actual teachings about worship, though we will draw upon both. Our greatest avenue for worship discipleship is becoming devoted followers of the worshiping Jesus through imitation.

Deliberating How Jesus Would Worship Today

Worship Discipleship

When someone comes to faith in Christ, discipleship is the next step. Most discipleship programs have concentrated on questions like these: How does a new believer learn to pray, read the Bible, share their faith, and serve others? Few discipleship plans have explicitly addressed the question "How does a new believer learn to worship God?" Yet this is the most urgent question, for worship lies at the heart of our relationship with God and the church. In fact, worship is the eternal point; it is the evidence that the mission of God has been completed when the new heaven and the new earth become the temple of God (Rev 21:1-5; 22). Ultimately, worship is the mission of God.

Unfortunately, discipling worshipers is often overlooked. Somewhere along the line we assumed that new believers would just catch on to proper worship by attending church. However, the risk of that approach is to assume that most people who attend church have been intentionally taught to worship God when they likely have not. Over time, without effective worship discipleship, it is possible to reproduce improper worship without meaning to do so.

Examples of Worship Discipleship (Biblical and Historical)

Worship discipleship is nothing new. It was a major theme throughout the Old Testament. For example, Moses insisted that Israel's elders intentionally instruct their children *throughout all generations* as to the meaning of the most profound worship event in their history—the Passover. Even before God's people had left Egypt, God instituted an annual worship ritual for every household to observe perpetually. The community was advised to take worship discipleship seriously: "You should observe this ritual as a regulation for all time for you and your children.... And when your children ask you, 'What does this ritual mean to you?' you will say, 'It is the Passover sacrifice to the LORD, for the LORD passed over the houses of the Israelites in Egypt. When he struck down the Egyptians, he spared our houses'" (Exod 12:24, 26-27). The very hearing of Moses's instructions became an occasion of worship: "The people then bowed down and worshiped" (Exod 12:27b). The emphasis upon worship discipleship in the Jewish faith is seen often throughout the Old Testament.[1]

Later on, during the early centuries of Christianity, the church developed a detailed plan to systematically disciple new believers in the Christian faith. A significant part of the program included educating believers as to the meaning of worship and instructing them in how to fulfill their very important role as a participant in worship. Their instruction included guidance in how to pray within the community, how to hear and receive the word of God preached, the meaning of one's baptism, the meaning of partaking of the Lord's table, and the relationship between worship and living lives of integrity and service.

This discipleship program, which eventually took several years for learners to complete, later came to be called the *catechumenate*[2] because teachers and students engaged in *catechesis*,[3] the process of instructing learners through oral means. (*Catechesis* means to give

7

instruction orally.)[4] The oral format took different forms over the centuries; but regardless of the form that was used, teachers vocalized words of instruction while the students let their teaching "resound in the ear and the heart."[5] Having received the teaching, learners allowed it to resonate within them and form them as they gained understanding that, in turn, helped them to become more faithful worshipers. Information resulted in formation.

In this ancient process, worship discipleship occurred as much through imitation as through oral instruction. Students would imitate the actions and the attitudes of their teachers in worship; they would then engage with the oral instruction in order to form their understanding. Imitation was followed by explanation; understanding followed action. This approach to discipleship is at the core of the early Christian model. Thus, the church carefully and systematically transmitted the teachings of the faith concerning worship (and other topics) as a means of Christian discipleship. In fact, *discipleship* was the very term preferred by the church fathers for this process.[6] From the beginning of the church and occurring through many centuries, new Christians were discipled first as worshipers.

From the beginning of the church, new Christians were discipled first as worshipers.

All Christian disciples are formed *in* worship *by* worship. The scriptures we hear, the songs we sing, the prayers we pray, the sermons we heed, the offerings we give, the Communion elements we share, the sense of love we feel from fellow worshipers—all of this and more unites in the power of the Spirit to change us toward Christlikeness. Worship is a highly transforming event. It is such a formational force that it is sometimes referred to as "primary theology"—the most significant occasion from which our understanding of God originates.

To be honest, for many years I had not considered how corporate worship is formational in nature. I had the idea that *I formed worship*; I have since discovered that *worship forms me*. I misunderstood the purposes of worship, thinking that it consisted largely of a service that people created in order to express themselves to God and to be inspired to live better Christian lives. It didn't occur to me that participating in the worship event is, in itself, an act of intentional spiritual formation. I have come to see that when worshipers participate faithfully and devotionally in the liturgy of their worship service (every church has its liturgy), they become deeply formed by what is said and done. Worship is a primary means through which our view of God and the world is reshaped in an ongoing way. But not only our *view* is changed. More importantly, through true worship our *affections*—that which/whom we come to love—are amended. Corporate worship disciples us in patterns of faith *and* patterns of love. The way of worship discipleship can be summarized this way: do as I do, come to believe what I believe, love what I love.

Current Challenge

Worship in local churches has changed a great deal over time, and most especially in the last fifty years in North America. In many places, worship would be virtually unrecognizable from that which took place even just a few years ago. Change can be good. Every generation must reconsider certain critical variables as they seek to worship God in their own time and place. But the question emerges: Who/what are we imitating when we adapt our practices of worship? Do worship practices find their source in the Teacher's way of worship? Or do we imitate another master?

In many churches, practices continue to migrate toward the latest cultural trends. Trends themselves are neither good nor bad until they are evaluated in terms of God's expectations for worship. However, it is wise to be cautious because we can inadvertently discover that we have chosen to imitate a person or a procedure or a product before asking, how would Jesus worship (HWJW)? Let me be clear at the beginning of this book. My concerns do not revolve around styles of worship. Sadly, battles over worship styles have so commonly been referred to as "worship wars" that everyone knows what the phrase means without explaining it. Whatever worship discipleship is, it rises above issues of style (though style considerations are not irrelevant). Often people will ask me, "What's next in worship?" That very question suggests that we are trend-thirsty. Too often we ask, "What's popular in worship today?" or "What would you like to see in worship?" or "What are the larger churches doing?"

I think it's time to ask the more relevant question: How would Jesus worship (HWJW)? If Jesus were present today, how *would* he worship? As this book unfolds chapter by chapter, we will take a look at this question from various vantage points and then draw implications for contemporary Christ-followers. We will do this because "the one who claims to remain in him ought to live in the same way as he lived" (1 John 2:6).

Do you hear the call—the call of Jesus? "Come follow me...in worship!"

Determining How I Will Worship

Reflection

After looking at our role model for worship, it's time to determine what adjustments our Master Teacher may be asking of his disciples. To begin, consider these questions:

- How do you think Jesus would worship today if he were here as before?

- Do you think he would alter his patterns and practices? If so, in what way?
- If I'm a disciple of Jesus, how willing am I to follow the Leader in worship?
- What might I have to do differently?
- What might I have to give up? Add on?
- How would my attitude change?
- How would my focus change?

Imagine

It's next Sunday. You've pulled into the parking lot at your church. You've walked through the door into the worship space. You remember that you are a learner and that Jesus is your role model for how you will worship right now.

- Identify one specific way that your approach to worship will be different than last Sunday.
- As you begin reading and studying this book, what invitation do you believe God is offering you personally as a follower of Jesus?
- As a result, what one concrete action step will you take this Sunday and every Sunday thereafter?

Action

With God's help, I determine that the next time I worship I will _____.

Prayer

Lord Jesus Christ,

Thank you for calling me to be your disciple. Help me to follow you in true worship discipleship. Send the Holy Spirit to strengthen me to be your follower. May God receive the glory.

Amen.

THE PRIORITY OF WORSHIP

KEY QUESTION:
HOW IMPORTANT WAS WORSHIP TO JESUS?

W e all have them—a little something called priorities—those things that consume our time and attention above other things. Our priorities can revolve around people, places, objects, or activities. We may prioritize certain persons in our lives by focusing on our friends, or spouse, or kids, or buddies from the weekend softball league. Sometimes places are a priority, such as the cabin in the woods, the beach, a local coffeehouse, favorite golf course, or the easy chair in front of the television. We can also prioritize objects like cars, sports memorabilia, antiques, or the next generation of tech toys.

A priority is a matter of regarding something or someone as more important than other available options. It is that to which we give the highest place in terms of our time, attention, and money. There have, no doubt, been times in your life when someone has asked you, "What are your priorities?" That's one way of asking, what do you value? Or perhaps you've heard it asked, "*Where* are your priorities?" Phrased this way, it sounds like priorities can be lost and then found. In a way, we can "lose" our priorities when they are misplaced; and we can "find" our priorities when we rediscover what should be important to us. The word *priority* is related to the word *prior*. A priority is that which is prior to all else.

What are your priorities in life? *Who* are your priorities in life?

Describing How We Worship Now

How Important Is Worship Anyway?

A few years ago, I was invited to speak to a large group of pastors at their annual continuing-education retreat. As I worked with the planning team in advance of the conference, I asked the team members (all pastors themselves), "What is the most urgent 'take-away' you hope for attendees to receive by the end of our time together?" Their response was immediate and crystal clear: "How can we help our parishioners to see the priority of worship for their faith, their lives, and their church?" They went on to explain that so many people view worship as something that good people just do—*good* people attend church. Most folks generally expect upstanding citizens to be churchgoers; going to church is part of being involved in the community, of performing one's civic duty, even a place for networking. The planning team knew that such a perspective had stripped their people of experiencing the true reality of corporate worship—of its power, its beauty, its urgency in the lives of believers, and its life-giving force to the ministries of the church. In short, their people had taken on a secular view of worship. The planning team concluded that it was no wonder that church attendance is in decline nationally. After all,

once Christians begin to believe that attending church is just one good activity among equally good options, choosing to join the family of faith in worship will no longer be a priority.

Part of the problem is that we use the word *worship* to refer to so many different things—popular religious music on inspirational radio, a contemporary musical style, worship concerts, personal devotions. We even mistakenly refer to it exclusively as the singing in worship. So at the outset, we need to clarify some terms.

What is *worship*? While there are many different and appropriate ways to speak of worship, this book is concerned with worship done in the context of the weekly gathering of God's people in an established community of faith recognized as an expression of "church." (This gathering may or may not occur in a church building.) It is about what is commonly called a "worship service"—a term with deep biblical and historical roots—as we meet to serve God and others through praise, prayer, song, word, and sacrament/ordinance,[1] and then continue our service in the world as an extension of our having been gathered and sent.

What is *corporate* worship? Corporate worship is worship done with and by members of the body of Christ who form the church. It is worship done in the physical presence of our Christian sisters and brothers, as opposed to private worship.

What is *Christian* corporate worship? It is the worship of the triune God, Father, Son, and Holy Spirit,[2] mediated by the continuing ministry of the Incarnate[3] Jesus. Christian corporate worship is worship that assumes the reality of the presence of the risen Lord Jesus Christ among the worshipers.

It took some time for corporate Christian worship to become the full-bodied entity that we now understand it to be. Inaugurated by the Holy Spirit and shaped by the church, we inherit worship that is rooted in ancient Jewish practices, boldly reinterpreted by the apostles, lovingly nurtured by the early church, and carefully articulated by a series of historic councils led by the church fathers. Our best understanding of worship is a glorious culmination of centuries of theological reflection.

Throughout this book the term *worship* will refer to Christian corporate worship. Let's define it:

Worship is the regular, ongoing meeting of a local body of Christian disciples with the triune God, expressed in acts of corporate devotion done in partnership with one another, in order to give glory to God, bear witness to their identity as God's people, proclaim and celebrate the grand narrative of God's eternal activity, and to receive power for living according to God's kingdom purposes.

Now that we are clear about how we are using the term *worship*, we can return to our question of priority. Just how important is worship anyway, not only for the Christian disciple but also for the church? To answer this question, we look to our Teacher.

How important was worship to Jesus?

Key Question: How important was worship to Jesus?

Discovering How Jesus Worshiped

Worshiping Like Jesus: Discovering His Priority

When people talk about Jesus, they often focus on his teachings and miracles as well as the key events of his earthly life—his birth, death, and resurrection. Yet a detailed reading of all four Gospels shows Jesus to be a very dedicated worshiper; it yields remarkable insights on just how much worship meant to Jesus. It might surprise you to learn that worship played the most profound role in Jesus's life. It is what proved to be the context for everything he taught, did, and experienced. In fact, once you see that the life of Jesus was a life of worship, it's impossible to speak of his ministry apart from Jesus the worshiper. When we discover just how much worship meant to him, everything else he did takes on new meaning. Worship was very important to Jesus. In fact, it was his priority.

Public Worship. First, public worship framed the beginning and the end of Jesus's earthly ministry. It began with a worship experience in the Jordan River. Jesus's baptism was the inaugural event that miraculously and publicly announced his identity as the Son of God, launching him into his upcoming years of sacrificial service in Palestine.

Jesus's baptism was a most significant occasion of worship: it occurred when Jesus had already assumed an attitude of worship and was praying (Luke 3:21-22); the trinitarian presence played an active role; it happened in the context of prophetic proclamation by John ("Prepare the way for the Lord!") followed by symbolic action (water baptism); and it was a religious ritual that the Prophet John had been called to administer from birth (see Luke 1:13-17). Though the sinless Jesus had no need of repentance and washing (the meaning of John's baptism), he entered into the waters as an act of obedience to the Father and to identify with those he came to serve. In so doing, he received both the Father's affirmation and the Spirit's confirmation, empowering him for ministry. It is inconceivable that Jesus would have considered undertaking his calling without this pivotal worship event, given that it demonstrated from the beginning that Jesus intended to "carry out all that God requires" (Matt 3:15 NLT). He did so as a worshiper.

Jesus's earthly ministry concluded with his ascension, another seminal event that occurred in the context of worship. After fulfilling everything that God had sent him to do, Jesus could have

simply disappeared from the disciples' sight without a word. Instead, acts of worship framed his return to heaven. Luke gives us a
detailed composite account (see Luke 24:50-53 and Acts 1:6-12).
Jesus called the eleven remaining disciples to a location well known
as his outdoor sanctuary of prayer, the Mount of Olives near
Bethany. There he announced the good news of the coming of the
Holy Spirit and advised them as to what this would mean; he lifted
his hands up in a gesture of blessing upon them and he pronounced
a benediction. Then, while in this very act of worship, Jesus was
carried up into heaven. And the worship continued: "They worshiped him and returned to Jerusalem overwhelmed with joy.
And they were continuously in the temple praising God" (Luke
24:52-53).

In these bookend events marking Jesus's earthly ministry, we find
that public worship was important to Jesus from the beginning to
the end. We will soon discover many examples of just how important
it was to Jesus throughout his lifetime.

Private Worship. As abundant as the evidence is of Jesus's commitment to public worship, we also see his similar commitment to
times of private worship. Jesus made private prayer a priority. He
often took off to the hills or some isolated place to be alone with God
in prayer (Mark 1:35; Matt 14:23). Jesus also consistently prayed in
critical times of decision or great crisis.[4] He prayed before calling the
twelve disciples (Luke 6:12-13), for Peter's faith before he denied
Jesus (Luke 22:31-34), for all present and future believers that they
would be kept from the evil one (John 17:15), for himself the night
before he was killed (Luke 22:42), and for his murderers while on
the cross (Luke 23:34).

I think you can see that it is just not possible to read the Gospels
and deduce that for Jesus, worship was an optional activity chosen
from among other activities. It wasn't something he participated in
when it was convenient. Quite the opposite. For Jesus, worship was
nothing less than an all-consuming, urgent, moment-by-moment
priority! Harold Best draws the same conclusion:

[Jesus's] earthly life was thirty-three years of unrelenting worship. He is the perfect worshiper, knowing his Father uninterruptedly, submissively and completely. In this sense Christ came to show us how Adam and Eve should have continued their worship. . . . Christ-on-earth, both God and image of God, both Creator and creature—this dearest of persons is a fully revealed picture of both how our unfallen parents should have continued to worship and how the body of Christ is eventually to worship.[5]

Deliberating How Jesus Would Worship Today

The Priority of Worship for the Church

Becoming worshipers of the one, true, triune God is the primary goal of all of God's initiatives, from creation to re-creation. Consequently, worship is the theme of all of scripture, from Genesis to Revelation. It is not inappropriate to say that the story line of scripture includes other central themes, such as covenant, or redemption, or justice, to name just a few. But what is the ultimate purpose of any of them? It is to produce worshipers of the living God. From beginning to end, God moves the created order toward ever-deepening expressions of developed praise and sacrificial worship. In fact, worship is the culmination of salvation history, as the Book of Revelation describes. (See Rev 5:11-14 and 19:6-8.) What began with intimate walks in the garden between God and the first two humans created (Gen 3:8) ends with a cacophony of glorious praise of myriads upon myriads of humans from all places and times—so many that no one can count—voicing loudly the sum of it all: "Salvation belongs to our God who is seated on the throne, and to the Lamb!" (Rev 7:10 NRSV). The worship of God is the whole point of God's story and therefore the primary theme of the entire scriptures. *Worship is the mission of God!*

Mission statements are very common today. Virtually all institutions, businesses, and even some individuals have unique mission statements. A mission statement essentially states clearly what the group or person hopes to accomplish as a result of their purpose. A purpose is *why* something exists; a mission is *what is done* as a result of its purpose.

Worship is the mission of God. That is to say, the worship of the one, true, triune God is the whole point of eternity. God has been and will be eternally worshiped. God was worshiped before there was time (before Creation), God made humans in God's image for relationship expressed in worship (Creation), and God will joyfully receive the worship of those redeemed by God's Son when the created order, as we know it now, comes to its intended conclusion and is re-made as a place of perfection for the purpose of worship (Re-Creation). What's more, all creation will be made new to participate in the re-created environment of worship in its own way. Creating and calling worshipers is what God is "up to" to fulfill God's purpose, which can be captured in one word: love. God *is* love. God's purpose is to invite those made in his image into the relationship of love he offers through Jesus Christ. God's purpose is love, and God's mission is inviting worshipers into receiving and participating in the relationship of love that he offers.

If worship is the mission of God, weekly worship in the context of a local church is the most important thing that the church does. It is at the center of our discipleship as followers of Jesus. It is the earthly expression of the eternal future. It is the bold, public witness of God's people that there is a God and that this true God meets with humans—the highest order of Creation—to gather them, speak to and hear from them, nourish them, and send them to proclaim the good news of God's love. God meets with them through and with the real presence of the Risen Lord Jesus Christ by the power of the Holy Spirit. Worship is the basis of our discipleship, the spiritual source for all of the ministries of the church with which we engage, and the way we express our unity with the worldwide Church, past, present, and future. It is no overstatement to say that worship's profound significance can be described as nothing less than urgent in its pressing priority: "Christian worship is the most momentous, the most urgent, the most glorious action that can take place in human life."[6]

Current Challenge

At the beginning of this chapter, a story was told of pastors who were concerned that their people held a mistaken view of the importance of worship. While you may view worship as a priority, there's a great chance that others in your congregation do not. In fact, that is just what some statistics indicate concerning the sobering worship attendance patterns of evangelical, mainline, and Catholic Christians:

- Fewer than 20 percent of Americans attend church on a given Sunday.[7]

- 23 to 25 percent of Americans attend church at least three out of every eight Sundays.[8]

- Most pastors report 40 to 60 percent of their membership is inactive.[9]

- Church attendance in America is steadily declining each decade.[10]

- 73 percent of Americans identify themselves as Christian and say religious faith is very important in their life;[11] yet when church attendance is added to these figures, the percentages dramatically decrease. In fact, the Barna Group now considers a person who attends church once per month to be categorized as a "practicing Christian."[12]

While Gallup polls report higher church attendance, by Gallup's admission, the results by Barna are likely more realistic once all factors are considered.[13] Another well-known research group, Pew Research

Center, reports similar results.[14] In short, there is a consistent consensus that church attendance is not a priority in America today.

So how important should corporate worship be to the Christian believer? How important is worship to the church? Should it be our priority? If so, how much of a priority? Prior to some things or prior to all things? Perhaps we should ask another important question: Who sets our priorities? Do we establish them or does someone else?

Worship Substitutes

Precisely due to declining church attendance, a number of "worship substitutes" have appeared on the scene to reimagine worship into something more attractive, with the hopes that these approaches could jump-start an upsurge in worship attendance. Here are a few worship substitutes that are commonly found in churches today:

- The program model. Functioning sort of like a Christian variety show, program worship consists of a sequence of entertaining acts that are performed on the stage to the delight of the audience. (Think celebrity interviews, exciting musical selections, special video presentations, performance artists, comedic preachers, etc.) Entertainment is the goal.

- The concert model. This music-driven model is delivered by way of a worship band performing popular Christian music for people to listen to and enjoy. Inspiration is the goal.

- The evangelistic model. Various nonreligious activities (raffles to win exotic gifts, free food and drink, product giveaways, etc.) are advertised in order to draw unchurched people in for the purpose of evangelization. Unsuspecting attendees may experience a sort of bait and switch campaign. Winning souls is the goal.

- The civic model. Guest speakers from the community or noted political figures are featured in worship to demonstrate the high visibility of the church in the community or to influence constituents in a certain social-political direction. This can take on the character of a secular rally rather than worship. Social engagement is the goal.

These activities can be good things to do—even recommended in the right context. But notice how far off course we can easily get if we begin to shape worship to serve marketing purposes in order to increase church attendance. These substitutes, or others like them, might draw a crowd, but they're not Christian worship as we will come to understand it. The weekly gathering of God's people for the express purpose of worshiping God is a meeting like no other! *This* event is different from any other religious gathering.

Often we feel pressure to take our cues from our context. If we're not careful, popular culture can influence our priorities without our realizing it. But our secular culture must not determine our priorities for us; we cannot look to the patterns of this world for the answer. Instead, we seek to "be transformed by the renewing of [our] minds so that [we] can figure out what God's will is—what is good and pleasing and mature" (Rom 12:2). Concerning worship, the way to begin to discern what is good and pleasing to God, and to mature in perspective, is to consult the scriptures, both Old and New Testaments, looking for principles of worship established by God. Most especially, since worship is a matter of our discipleship in following Jesus, how Jesus prioritized worship when he was on earth really matters. Franklin Segler stated it well:

> God will be served for God's glory alone, not as a means to an end.... Worship, not church growth, must be the church's priority. At all costs churches must resist the temptation to embrace all cultural norms and innovative worship forms without first considering how God will be honored.[15]

If we view worship today as programs or concerts or evangelization or civic opportunities, we will have lost our priorities. We need to find them again. We cannot co-opt worship to serve other purposes and please God. A. W. Tozer states it well: "Worship is no longer worship when it reflects the culture around us more than the Christ within us."[16] Only when we see true worship for what it really is from God's point of view, through the lens of Jesus, will we rediscover our true and highest priority.

The faithful worship of believers assembled as the church before God must become the highest priority of the Christian life. We make it a priority not to be legalistic, or to report better attendance statistics, or because we feel pressure from denominational leaders, or to compete with other churches. It becomes a priority on its own terms—not because it *should be* but because it *must be*. And the reason it *must be* a priority is because we are serious disciples of Jesus, who modeled worship as his priority precisely because he understood God's love of and purposes in worship.

How would Jesus worship (HWJW)? He would worship as if it were the most important thing in his life. Do you hear the call—the call of Jesus? "Come follow me…in making worship a high priority!"

HWJW? Jesus would worship as if it was the most important thing in his life.

Determining How I Will Worship

Reflection

After looking at Jesus, our role model for worship, it's time to determine what adjustments our Master Teacher may be asking of his disciples. To begin, consider these questions:

- Reflect upon your habit of worship attendance. How has it changed over the years? What, if anything, calls you away from weekly worship?

- Does corporate worship mark the basic rhythm of your life? (Is worship the high point of your week, from which your daily life flows?)

- If you attend worship very regularly, in what other ways could you improve upon making it a priority in your life? (For example, making spiritual and mental preparation for worship prior to the service? Reading and contemplating the scripture readings for worship in advance? Going to bed at a reasonable time on Saturday evening? Praying for the body of worshipers and its leaders throughout the week? Inviting others to join you in worship?)

- Think about the many different ways that Jesus was engaged in worship during his lifetime. Which aspect really speaks to you today? Why?

- Have you ever written a personal mission statement? If so, what is it? How might you adjust it after studying Jesus's priority for worship?

- What challenges you the most when you think about making worship a high priority?

- What would it look like for you to take the next step in making corporate worship a greater priority in your life?

Imagine

It's next Saturday. Your friend calls and invites you to spend the next day fishing. You start to say yes. It would be fun. Besides, you go to church 50 percent of the time. Enough other people will be there. Then you remember that it's not about quotas; it's about following Jesus in making corporate worship a priority. You decide to speak to your friend about finding an alternative day to go fishing.

- Identify one specific way that you could begin making worship a higher priority in your life.

- What one concrete action step will you take right now to fulfill your commitment this Sunday and every Sunday thereafter?

Action

With God's help, I determine to make worship a greater priority by _____. (Be specific.)

Prayer

Dear God,

Fill my heart with a singular desire to make worship the top priority of my life. Help me not to view worship as a duty, but as a great blessing and privilege. May I not use worship to serve my own purposes. Instead, help me to offer worship freely to serve your purposes. Through Christ our Lord, Amen.

Chapter 3

THE OBJECT OF WORSHIP

KEY QUESTION:
WHOM DID JESUS WORSHIP?

O ne of the earliest game shows on television was *To Tell the Truth.* First airing in 1956, it has had an impressive run over the course of more than six decades, being broadcast by three different major networks and then in syndication. Even today the show is introduced to a new audience with yet another updated version appearing on a major television network.

The point of the show is the panelists' ability to tell truth from falsehood. One contestant, having accomplished something noteworthy, is to "tell the truth" concerning their achievement while two impostors pretend to be this same person. Famous celebrities attempt to decide who is telling the truth and who are the impostors by asking questions of the three people who claim to be the real person of note. After the questions have concluded, the game show host asks, "Will the real [name] please stand up?" The moment of truth has arrived, and the people's identities are revealed—one is true and the others are false. The intrigue of the game is that it can be downright difficult to tell which of the three persons is the real deal. Any or all of the contestants appear convincing, but only one is telling the truth. Discerning between truth and falsehood can be a real challenge. The more counterfeit options there are, the more difficult it becomes.

Describing How We Worship Now

When it comes to worship, the most important determination one can make is which god to worship. Like the television host of *To Tell the Truth*, we ask, "Will the real God please stand up?" Whom you will worship is the most critical question to be asked and answered as a disciple of Jesus. It is the eternal question—the one that began in the garden of Eden (serpent or God?) and ends in the New Jerusalem (the beast or God?).[1] From Genesis to Revelation, the answer to the most important question of the cosmos—whom will you worship—has one answer: the one true God as revealed in scripture. There are a lot of variables as to how people worship, but for the Christian there is no variable as to whom is worshiped. What's more, not only do we worship this God, we worship this God and this God alone.

It may seem obvious that the object of our worship is God. Yet today, "God" can mean very different things to different people—even people who have been in church a long time. It is no longer realistic to assume that everyone who goes to church clearly understands who God is. Clarifying just exactly who is the God of scripture is becoming more of a necessity due to expanding religious opinions that blur the lines. With the fast-paced and worldwide communications capabilities today, religious opinions spread rapidly. Isn't one god the same as another? Does it really matter which god you believe in as long as you believe in some god? Adding to the confusion is the notion that any religion would even suggest that their god is the only god to be worshiped.

See if you can recognize any of the ways that modern thinking tends to muddy the waters when considering the object of our worship.

God PLUS. It is fine to worship the God of scripture, but you may also worship other gods at the same time that may be convenient to your situation—for instance, while visiting or living in another culture. This is *polytheistic worship* (worshiping more than one god at once).

God MINUS. Meeting God's expectations for true worship is good if possible, but not a necessity. God just wants worshipers to be happy, so whatever or however they go about it is OK. God's fine when we're just there doing our best. Worshipers are content with "God lite" worship as long as it is pleasing to them. This is *narcissistic worship* (worship focused on our own pleasure).

God OR. It doesn't matter which god you worship as long as you believe in a god. Worshipers may choose a deity based on what makes sense to them. Just pick one. Truth is relative. This is *relativistic worship* (one god is as good as another).

God VAGUE. There are alternative titles sometimes used for God that leave the worshiper quite open to interpret just who this God is. If God is referred to in such terms as Universal One, Higher Power, Radiant One, and so on, it can get confusing. When titles for God are vague, they provide lots of room to interpret the character and nature of God according to one's human perspective.[2] This is *ambiguous worship* (God is defined in unparticular ways).

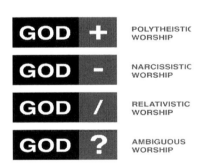

GOD +   POLYTHEISTIC WORSHIP

GOD −   NARCISSISTIC WORSHIP

GOD /   RELATIVISTIC WORSHIP

GOD ?   AMBIGUOUS WORSHIP

It is easy to see the widespread confusion on the landscape today concerning the recipient of worship. That's why the object of our worship must be clearly identified. If our goal is to follow Jesus as his disciples, we must ask this most important question: Whom did Jesus worship?

29

Discovering How Jesus Worshiped

Worshiping Like Jesus: Whom Did Jesus Worship?

Whom did Jesus worship? All four Gospel writers portray the worshiping Jesus with a singular focus: Jesus worshiped God and God alone. In this section we will first examine whom Jesus worshiped (God); then we will look at the exclusive nature of Jesus's worship (God alone).

Jesus Worshiped God

Jesus could not be clearer about the object of his worship: he worshiped God. Every instance of Jesus as a worshiper—in the temple, in the synagogue, in public prayer, in private prayer—depicts him as worshiping God. But which God in particular? After all, in the Roman culture that permeated Palestine, there were dozens of gods being worshiped where Jesus lived.

Jesus worshiped the one true God who was revealed in the great tradition of his inherited faith of many centuries. The God Jesus worshiped was the eternal, triune God of Creation, the God of Abraham, the God of Moses, the God of the patriarchs, the prophets, the kings, and the God of his human parents, Joseph and Mary.

The God of Jesus's Jewish tradition became the backdrop for what perhaps is Jesus's most significant, straightforward teaching on worship. John 4:1-30 records a fascinating encounter between an unnamed Samaritan woman and Jesus. While there are many intriguing dimensions to discover throughout the encounter, we will limit our discussion to the conversation about worship, which is at the heart of the story (vv. 19-26). In fact, some New Testament scholars have argued that the very purpose of John's Gospel is to bring people to the right worship of God.[3]

The conversation took place at Jacob's well, a shared historical site for both Samaritans and Jews. Samaritans (of partial Jewish descent) and Jews (of full Jewish descent) had long-standing bad blood. John clues us in: "Jews do not share things in common with Samaritans" (John 4:9b NRSV). So it is ironic that this event occurred at a site of historical value that they *did* share in common. Jacob's well was dug long before any of the social and cultural divisions that came later. Two people who seemingly had nothing in common—they did not associate with each other—end up in a conversation at a place of common heritage due to their common ancestor. However, sharing a drink of cool water at a shared historical location led to the sharing of so much more.

Within this conversation about worship there are a lot of particular questions that emerged: where, when, how? The woman seemed quite interested in *where* worship should occur—the mountain in Samaria or Jerusalem? Jesus seemed interested in discussing *when*; twice he emphasized, "The time is coming" (vv. 21, 23). *How* to worship—in spirit and in truth—is a big part of the conversation too. (In chapter 6 we will return to this part of the story to examine the "how" question in depth.) But the most important question discussed was *who*: who is to be worshiped? Jesus was very clear in his words to the woman: "You and your people will worship the Father" (v. 21). Jesus further emphasized that the Father is worshiped by stating that the Father seeks worshipers (v. 23).

While on earth, Jesus as a human being worshiped the Father. This Father-Son bond formed the essence of their relationship, made clear at his baptism. To Jesus, God was Father. What's more, because Jesus is still incarnate—still God in the flesh—he continues to worship the Father. (We will discover in the next chapter that both Christ and the Holy Spirit are worthy recipients of worship also.) Ultimately, we worship a trinitarian God as hinted at in the story when Jesus mentions that the time is coming—in fact, it is here with the arrival of the Messiah, when true worshipers will worship in spirit (Spirit) and truth (v. 23).[4] I know: it's a glorious mystery! But that's OK. After all, "mystery is not a puzzle to be solved but a truth to be reverenced."[5]

The first part of the answer to our question, whom did Jesus worship, is this: Jesus worshiped God, the God revealed to his ancestors, who was also the God who called him Son.

Jesus Worshiped God and God Alone

Jesus worshiped God, but he took it a step further; he would worship God alone. God was the sole object of Jesus's worship. His resolve was tested at the earliest point of his earthly ministry. Apparently it was the one thing he had to get right from the very beginning. Would he worship God *exclusively*? Immediately following his baptism he was led by the Spirit into the desert to be tempted by the devil. Here was Jesus's first real test. Would he pass the test? The tempter had tricks up his sleeve. They included this one: "Then the devil brought him to a very high mountain and showed him all the kingdoms of the world and their glory. He said, 'I'll give you all these if you bow down and worship me.'

"Jesus responded, 'Go away, Satan, because it's written, *You will worship the Lord your God and serve only him*'" (Matt 4:8-10). Jesus's response directly reflected the foundational teachings of his historic faith (see Deut 6:13). In choosing to quote Moses, the first and greatest leader of God's covenant people, Jesus was drawing an unbroken line between the one true God of Israel who alone was to be worshiped and the God he pledged to worship exclusively as well. In this exchange between Jesus and the devil, Jesus was not only indicating whom he *would* worship; he was also declaring whom he would *not* worship. His unrelenting commitment to worship the Lord God alone was an act of defiance against the evil one. Likewise, every time a Christian worships the one true God, they are not only establishing whom they will worship, but also whom they will not worship. Every true act of Christian worship is in defiance of Satan—the one who has contended for God's glory from before the creation of the world (see Isa 14:12-15 and Luke 10:18). The stakes were very high for Jesus the worshiper; they are equally high for every Christian. Jesus stood his test. As his followers, so must we.

Another way that we see Jesus exclusively worshiping God is in his life of prayer. Jesus prayed solely to God. In particular, he favored praying to his Father—a unique practice—for "Jews rarely addressed God as *Father*, but Jesus did so in every prayer but one (Mark 15:34)."[6] He also passed this practice on to his disciples in teaching them (and us) to pray likewise, "Our Father who is in heaven…" (Matt 6:9). Prayer is an act of worship; we pray to the one we worship. On the many occasions of prayer throughout the Gospels, Jesus addressed God and God alone.

When it comes to whom we should worship, our Teacher was faithful to God and his own community of ancient faith by honoring the first commandment given in the Law of Moses that has echoed throughout the scriptures from beginning to end: "I am the Lord your God. … You must have no other gods before me" (Exod 20:2-3). Jesus worshiped God and God alone.

Deliberating How Jesus Would Worship Today

Christian worship has a singular object: the triune God as revealed in holy scripture. God is the object of our worship, not only because the Law says so, but because God's love says so. Love is the reason for the Law. Biblical worship is focused upon the object of our love, not the object of a legal code.

So what does God-focused worship mean?

- It means that God initiates worship as the central means of relationship between God and God's people, and that worship unfolds as we respond to God's call to worship together.

- It means that the presence of God is the preeminent reality of worship.

- It means that we are preoccupied with God when we worship—that we discipline our thoughts Godward, that we lay aside distractions that may turn our attention away from worship.

- It means that God's story reveals God's glory. The grand narrative of all of God's work—past, present, and future—properly orients our actions in worship to proclaim and celebrate what God has done, is doing, and will do.

- It means that God is the beginning and the middle and the end of Christian worship.

- It means that we adjust our vision to behold God in God's beauty, holiness, truth, and goodness. Like playing with a kaleidoscope, corporate worship is the great opportunity to adjust the lens, to overcome the fuzzy chaos of our lives and await the distinct and beautiful image of God to appear.

- Most of all, to worship is to express devotion to God, the object of our love.

God is the object of worship but God is also the subject of worship (the one who does the action). Robert Webber summarizes God's action in worship in striking terms:

> One of the greatest discoveries of my Christian pilgrimage has come with the realization that the primary importance in worship is not what *I* do but what *God* is doing. In worship, God is present, speaking to me, and acting upon me. It is in worship that God feeds, nourishes, and cares for me. And it is in worship that he gives me his grace, surrounds me with his love, lifts me up into his arms, affirms me as a member of his community, and sends me forth into the world with a fresh vision of his work and a new concern to live for him.[7]

God is both object and subject. God is all in all. Worship begins and ends with God.

Current Challenge

We face some challenges in embracing God as the sole object of worship. A. W. Tozer stated the case bluntly: "It is scarcely possible in most places to get anyone to attend a meeting where the only attraction is God."[8] For many years church leaders have felt the increasing pressure of whether or not the presence of God is perceived to be enough to draw people to church. To counter this fear, some churches have responded with various approaches meant to attract people. In so doing, they have sometimes shifted from God as the object of worship to people as the consumers of worship. However, when the focus of our worship shifts from God-directed worship to people-pleasing worship, biblical worship can be quickly compromised. God is always the primary focus (in relationship with his people). Consider this challenge:

What comes into our minds when we think about God is the most important thing about us…[as] no religion has ever been greater than its idea of God. Worship is pure or base as the worshiper entertains high or low thoughts of God….Always the most revealing thing about the Church is her idea of God, just as her most significant message is what she says about him or leaves unsaid, for her silence is often more eloquent than her speech.[9] To come full circle, while traveling through Samaria, Jesus spoke of true worship. True worship stands over against false worship.

True worship involves…

- worshiping the right object: God and God alone;
- through the right means: prayer, adoration, word, table, song, and so on;
- with the right attitude and intentions: humility, reverence, and joy.

False worship involves…

- worshiping the wrong object: culture, self, church growth, and so on;

35

- through the wrong means: emotionalism, consumerism, entertainment, and so on;
- with the wrong attitude: self-serving, proud, competitive.

HWJW Today?

If Jesus were here today, and we asked him this question—whom should we worship?—his response would be eager and direct: We must worship God and God alone. In a world where it is less and less obvious that there is one true God to be worshiped above all others, we must follow our Teacher's example. Do you hear the call of Jesus? "Come, follow me in worshiping God and God alone."

Determining How I Will Worship

Reflection

After looking at Jesus, our role model for worship, it's time to determine what adjustments our Master Teacher may be asking of his disciples. To begin, consider these questions:

- How significant a role has your formal faith tradition (your church) and/or your family's Christian faith tradition played in clearly identifying the God you worship?

- Review the types of worship described in the first part of this chapter: polytheistic, narcissistic, relativistic, ambiguous. Have you ever seen any of these in worship?

- If you could have secretly listened in to Jesus's discussion with the Samaritan woman, what would be the most important thing you would have learned about worship?

- Like Jesus in the wilderness, if someone invited you to worship a false god, how would you respond? Has this ever happened to you? If so, how *did* you respond?

- What challenges you the most when you think about worshiping God and God alone?

Imagine

It's next Sunday. As you leave for church you remember that there are some Christian believers in other parts of the world who are imprisoned for worshiping God and God alone.

- What prayer will you offer for them as they worship God while suffering for doing so? What prayer will you offer for yourself as you worship freely? What prayer will you offer for your own worshiping community that is gathering?

- Formulate your own one-sentence creed that proclaims whom you intend to worship now and always. Repeat this creed weekly on the way to worship.

Action

What commitments are you willing to make as you consider whom you will worship? With God's help, I resolve to worship God and God alone by _____. (Be specific.)

Prayer

Holy Spirit,

Purify my commitment to worshiping the triune God as the sole object of my affection. Show me where there may be any falsehoods that have crept into my worship practices of which I am unaware. Set my heart on a new path toward worshiping God and God alone. Through Christ, I pray.

Amen.

Chapter 4

THE CENTRAL FIGURE OF WORSHIP

KEY QUESTION:
WHAT ARE CHRIST'S UNIQUE ROLES IN WORSHIP?

Every organized group with a purpose has a key leader—
someone who helps all of the members of the organization
to play their part so that the purpose of the group is fulfilled. Leaders play multifaceted roles because many dimensions of
leadership are needed in order for the group to truly succeed.

Think, for example, of an athletic coach. A coach is a leader who
plays many different roles all at once as needed by the team. Coaches
strategize for the best use of each team member, putting them in
the spot where they can flourish. They train each player in the skills
needed for their unique position, develop a game plan, provide positive motivation, and keep the big picture and long-range plans for
the team in perspective. In a similar way, a school principal leads a
team of educators while serving them in a variety of roles. Principals
place teachers at the level for which they are best suited, evaluate
their classroom performance, build morale within the faculty, ar-
range for the best use of the physical property, serve as a liaison between parents and teachers, advocate for classroom support, and inspire their teachers to keep the main thing the main thing. Whatever
the organization—a church, a civic club, an orchestra—someone is

appointed to give key direction to all of the parts. That person fulfills many roles at once in serving the members of the group.

When we gather to worship God as a local congregation, usually one or more key leaders help people to play their part. It may be a pastor, or another worship leader, or a team of leaders. Whoever it is, someone helps to organize and inspire worshipers. The human leaders are the visible presence that provides key leadership to help worship happen. But the interesting thing is this: there is really someone else who is serving a significant, multifaceted role that is unseen yet indispensible to the success of worship. That person is Jesus Christ.

Describing How We Worship Now

Throughout this book we are looking primarily at how Jesus was a worshiper. Along the way we are also discovering what Jesus taught others about worship from time to time. In chapter 4, however, we must step out of this approach and look at worship from a different angle to notice what the scriptures and the church teach about Christ's role when believers assemble to worship. For this one chapter, Jesus will not speak for himself; rather, we will focus on what we know about the Incarnate Christ[1] as a result of faithful teaching.

Jesus has a dual nature; he is at once both divine and human. As a human, Jesus is a worshiper. Therefore, we can follow him in discipleship as worshipers. As divine, Jesus is worshiped. He never proclaimed himself to be the centerpiece of worship—quite the opposite, as Paul asserts: "Though [Jesus] was in the form of God, he did not consider being equal with God something to exploit" (Phil 2:6). Rather, it was God the Father's idea to position the Son to be the center of worship: "Therefore, God highly honored him and gave him a name above all names, so that at the name of Jesus everyone in heaven, on earth, and under the earth might bow and every tongue confess that Jesus Christ is Lord, to the glory of God the Father"

40

(Phil 2:9-11). We must therefore look to God's divine plan to determine what unique roles Christ plays in relation to worship.

Just before we discover these roles, however, we must first of all affirm Christ's presence within the Christian community when it gathers to worship. Whatever role Christ fulfills rests upon our belief that he is with us as one of us in worship. This is the essential starting place in understanding everything else. When the church meets for worship, the person of Christ is present—really present.

Though we cannot visibly see Christ, he is nevertheless there. The reality of his presence does not depend upon us seeing him—he is there whether we see him or miss him—but we must come to recognize the promise of his presence as a vital reality. After his resurrection, Jesus mystically appeared to his disciples. Sometimes they recognized him; other times they did not, yet he was there, nonethe-

less. On the morning of the resurrection, Mary Magdalene lived in this tension of failing to recognize Jesus (John 20:14) yet worshiping him (Matt 28:9). On the evening of the resurrection, the disciples from Emmaus likewise did not recognize Jesus at first, but came to experience his presence at the breaking of the bread (Luke 24:15-16, 30-31, 35). Similarly, our resurrected Lord is present in worship, unseen but truly with us. Sometimes we recognize him; other times we do not due to our own preoccupations. Either way, it does not change the reality that Jesus is with us in worship.

Christ's real presence in worship is assured to us in several New Testament passages. The author of Hebrews quotes Jesus speaking to God: *I will praise you in the middle of the assembly.* He also says, *Here I am with the children whom God has given to me* (Heb 2:11b-13). Also,

Paul strongly implies the presence of the Lord Jesus in worship when he writes to the church at Corinth. In 1 Corinthians 5:4 he refers to assembling "in the name of our Lord Jesus" where there is also "the power of our Lord Jesus." Paul is claiming that believers meeting in the name of Jesus for worship assume the power and presence of the Lord Jesus. Surely he is recollecting how Jesus himself promised, "For where two or three are gathered in my name, I'm there with them" (Matt 18:20). Earlier in his letter, Paul instructs the believers that "you" (plural) are the temple of God in which the Spirit of God dwells (1 Cor 3:16). *Collectively*, the Spirit of God (which is the Spirit of Christ) dwells in us. Therefore when we meet collectively, the Spirit of Christ is present.

Recognizing and celebrating the presence of the risen Lord Jesus Christ as we worship is the most profound reality we can discover about worship. This one realization holds the potential to revitalize worship in every context. It makes all the difference in the world! The stage is now set to ask what his presence really means to us:

What are Christ's unique roles in worship?

Key Question: What are Christ's unique roles in worship?

Discovering How Jesus Worshiped

There are at least three very significant roles that Christ plays in Christian worship: Christ receives our worship, Christ mediates our worship, and Christ leads our worship.

Christ Receives Our Worship

First, Christ receives our worship. He does so because he is God. Here is where our understanding of the dual nature of Christ is vital. On one hand, how is it possible for Jesus, who is God, to be a worshiper? On the other hand, how does Jesus, as a human, receive worship? This is a complex idea—so complex that it took hundreds of years and six official councils of the church to ultimately sort it out: Jesus was at once *both* fully human and fully divine. When Jesus was born, the Son of God appeared in a human body; he was given skin and bones. To be clear, Jesus was *fully* human, made with a body, soul, and mind—just like each of us. In his *human* nature he is less than God. He had human limitations. That is why Jesus's life of worshiping the Father was possible; Jesus was a human worshiper who worshiped God. At the same time, his *divine* nature was fully God. As divine, Jesus was neither less than God nor greater than God, but equal with God the Father and God the Holy Spirit as a full member of the Trinity. That is why Jesus is also eligible to receive worship.

The miracle of the Incarnation joined the human and divine natures of Jesus into one. He is not two separate halves, but one being with two natures simultaneously. The second chapter of Philippians, mentioned above, is eloquently written from the perspective of the Incarnate Christ. Both dimensions of Christ are portrayed at once: (1) he is a worshiper who did not seek equality with God but willingly condescended to be born as a human (vv. 6-8), and (2) at the same time he is worshiped because God highly exalted him to receive the worship of every other created being (vv. 9-11). What's more, because he is still the Incarnate Christ, Jesus in his human nature continues to worship the Father, while the Divine Christ continues to receive worship also. The magnificent sum of it all is this: Jesus is the worshiped worshiper![2]

Jesus is the worshiped worshiper.

I know. It's another great mystery. But remember, just because a concept can't be entirely explained doesn't mean that it is not true; it simply means that our finite minds can't fully comprehend the infinite. Every religion requires faith of its members. Our faith to believe is given to us as a gift from the Spirit to believe the fundamental truths of our religion.

The scriptures note that Jesus received worship from others—from the blind man healed (John 9:38), from the disciples in the boat after he calmed the storm (Matt 14:33), from Mary Magdalene and the other Mary who worshiped at Jesus's feet when he met them early in the morning the day of the Resurrection (Matt 28:9), and also from Thomas, who worshiped Jesus with his striking exclamation, "My Lord and my God!" (John 20:28). At his ascension the disciples worshiped him yet again (Luke 24:52; Matt 28:17). On no occasion did Jesus dismiss loving gestures of outright adoration.

After Jesus's ascension and into the earliest days of the church, Jesus Christ continued to receive worship. Larry Hurtado, a scholar of the early church, affirms that Jesus was corecipient of devotion (with God) by the earliest Christians—a most radical development, given Judaism's insistence of worshiping only one God. He notes that prayer is offered through and to Jesus, acts of worship are directed toward Jesus, Jesus is confessed to be Lord, Jesus is sung to devotionally in worship, and more.[3] Over the centuries, Christ's role as recipient of worship is one of the primary articles of the Christian faith.[4] What's more, it is the worship of Christ that will be the grand climax of the story when God puts all things under his feet (1 Cor 15:25) and the heavenly beings once again sing with full voice, "Worthy is the Lamb that was slaughtered to receive power and wealth and wisdom and might and honor and glory and blessing!" (Rev 5:12 NRSV).

With the attention on God the Son in worship, you may wonder about the Holy Spirit's role. God the Holy Spirit plays a vital role in Christian worship that is sometimes overlooked or at least understated, which is unfortunate. The Holy Spirit is always present and active when the community gathers to worship. Indeed, it is by the Spirit's power that worship even occurs. We can't worship without the Spirit's help. The Spirit's presence enlivens the members of the community and empowers them according to their spiritual gifts so as to contribute to worship. But most of all, the Spirit helps worshipers to truly see and experience the presence of the risen Lord. The Spirit is given to remind believers of all that Jesus has said (John 14:26) and to testify on Jesus's behalf (John 15:26). Indeed, it is by the Holy Spirit, the Spirit of Truth, that our eyes are opened and we recognize Jesus (John 14:17).

The coeternal Persons of the Godhead are always involved as one in the sweeping initiatives of the triune God: Creation, Incarnation, Redemption, Re-Creation, and so on. Yet often, one figure plays the lead role with the others serving as vital coparticipants. No initiative of God is done without the partnership of the Triune Being. At no point do any Persons of the Godhead feel slighted or jealous in any way while one or the other takes the lead. Their actions depict a perfect circle dance with one taking the lead here and another there.[5] The three Persons of the Godhead are perfect in love, purpose, deference, and community.

At its core, worship is trinitarian. God the Father, God the Son, and God the Spirit are always active participants in worship, playing their vital roles. However, to serve God's purposes, Jesus Christ is at the center of Christian worship past, present, and future. Our fear that exalting Christ in worship might throw the Divine Being out of balance is simply that—*our* unfounded fear. We may find ourselves keeping score to make sure that all persons are equal in prominence. If so, that is a matter of us reading into the situation from our human perspective, not considering the divine perspective as it is found in the scriptures and the earliest believers. Ultimately, trinitarian worship is Christocentric worship. One does not contradict the other.

So to be crystal clear, all Persons of the Trinity receive worship, individually and as One God. It is certainly biblical to worship God! But Jesus Christ is set forth as the undeniable object of devotion through which God is glorified. Bryan Chapell states the significance of Christ-centered worship clearly: "The heart of Christian worship is love for Christ. We cannot love him without extolling his greatness, confessing our weakness, seeking his goodness, thanking him for his grace, and living for his glory. So, out of love for him, we worship him in these ways."⁶ It is more than fitting to worship the triune God through Jesus Christ. In fact, we must, for that is the will of God for us.

Christ Mediates Our Worship

Second, Christ mediates our worship. Worship offered to God without divine assistance would fall short of God's purposes. Our own qualifications to offer worship are inadequate. Humanly orchestrated worship can't stand on its own merit. Frankly, we need divine intervention in worship; we need a mediator.

A mediator is someone who stands in the middle between two parties who are separated and in need of being brought together. *Mediation* is a commonly used term for the process of resolving an impasse such as a contract dispute between employer and employees, broken family relationships, international conflicts, and so on. A mediator attempts to reconcile persons. (Even our road system includes *medians*—land in the middle of lanes of traffic to reconcile opposing traffic flow.)

The scriptures teach that there is "one mediator between God and humanity, the human Christ Jesus" (1 Tim 2:5). As such, he stands in the middle between God and people to bridge the gap in so many ways: as the mediator who provides redemption (Heb 7:25; 9:15), as the mediator in prayer (Heb 7:25), and yes, as mediator of our worship. Think about it. Christ brings God and people together to worship!

In the Old Testament, the high priest mediated worship. Offering sacrifices ordained by God, he stood in the middle between God and the covenant people. Worship without the high priest's mediation was not acceptable to God. But in the unfolding of God's wonderful plan, we now have Jesus to serve as our high priest: "holy, innocent, incorrupt, separate from sinners, and raised high above the heavens" (Heb 7:26). Jesus, the once-and-for-all sacrifice, is qualified to stand "in the middle of the assembly" (Heb 2:12) making our worship acceptable to God. Jesus leads in two-way worship between the community and God. He speaks to God *for* us and he offers praises back to God *with* us. What a remarkable reality! And Jesus, still the God-man, is the only one who is qualified to fill this role. Theologian James B. Torrance says it in a way that fills us with wonder:

> Jesus comes to be the priest of creation to do for us, men and women, what we failed to do, to offer to the Father the worship and the praise we failed to offer.... Jesus comes as our brother to be our great high priest.... He comes to stand in for us in the presence of the Father, when in our failure and bewilderment we do not know how to pray as we ought to, or forget to pray altogether.... Christ takes what is ours (our broken lives and unworthy prayers), sanctifies them, offers them without spot or wrinkle to the Father, and gives them back to us, that we might "feed" upon him in thanksgiving. He takes our prayers and makes them his prayers, and he makes his prayers our prayers, and we know our prayers are heard "for Jesus' sake."[7]

What an incredible role Jesus plays in sanctifying our worship so that it is acceptable to God. Worship isn't possible without our Mediator.

Christ Leads Our Worship

Third, Christ leads our worship. The book of Hebrews refers to Jesus with that very Greek term, *leitourgos*, which means "the leader of our worship" (Heb 8:2). Christ is our liturgist—the one who facilitates the prayers and praises of the community as it offers worship to God. Jesus does not lead worship from a distance; he leads as one of us! He calls us family, for he "isn't ashamed to call [us] brothers and sisters" (Heb 2:11b). He takes his place among us, declaring, *Here I am with the children whom God has given to me* (Heb 2:13b). Jesus belongs to the community of worship. How spectacular to think that

47

the risen Lord not only receives and mediates our worship, but also leads it.

It's an amazing reality; Jesus Christ is the recipient, the mediator, and the leader of our worship! Only the Incarnate Christ is perfectly capable of performing all of these necessary functions of Christian worship at once. This fantastic truth should infuse our worship with new joy and strength. We are not on our own to make worship happen. It is already happening; we just have the fantastic privilege of joining Christ as participants in his worship of the Father!

Deliberating How Jesus Would Worship Today

I often wonder whether churches truly believe Jesus is present when we worship. Maybe that's why we work so hard at producing services that we hope will attract a crowd as we compete with whatever else holds greater appeal in today's world.

C. S. Lewis tried to warn us of this danger in his classic book *The Screwtape Letters*. There are three main characters: Uncle Screwtape (a higher demon), Wormwood (his nephew, who is a demon in training), and the Enemy (God). Screwtape writes a series of letters to Wormwood, advising him in the fine art of deceiving Christians. In one of his letters, Screwtape writes,

My dear Wormwood,

Work on the horror of the Same Old Thing.... [It] is one of the most valuable passions we have produced in the human heart... [the] demand for absolute novelty. This demand is entirely our workmanship.... This demand is valuable [to us] in various ways. In the first place it diminishes pleasure while increasing desire. The pleasure of novelty is by its very nature more subject than any other to the law of diminishing returns. And continued novelty costs money, so that the desire for it spells avarice or unhappiness or both.

[The Enemy] wants people, so far as I can see, to ask very simple questions; is it righteous? Is it prudent? Is it possible? Now if we can keep [them] asking, "Is it in accordance with the general movement of our time? Is it progressive ...? Is this the way that History is going?" they will neglect the relevant questions ... As a result, while their minds are buzzing in this vacuum, we have the better chance to slip in and bend them to the action *we* have decided on. And great work has already been done.

Your affectionate uncle,

Screwtape[8]

Current Challenges

When I read Lewis's words, I think of worship. Let me paraphrase: God wants people, so far as I can see, to ask very simple questions; is worship righteous, biblical, Christ-centered? If we can keep people asking other questions—is our worship in accordance with the general movement of our time? Is it progressive? Is this the way culture is going?—they will neglect the relevant questions. And as a result, when they are preoccupied with the wrong set of questions, we have a better chance to slip in and bend the actions of worship in the direction *we* have decided upon.

There is some indication that, indeed, "great work has already been done." Perhaps that's why I hear of churches that are preoccupied with that which is novel, churches that:

- Sell raffle tickets for the possibility of winning a Jeep Grand Cherokee on a special Sunday morning.

- Hold a contest for who can do the most push-ups on stage, with the winner earning the right to sit in a massage chair while the preacher preaches.

- Transform the floor seating area of their church into a rodeo ring—complete with sawdust—so the pastor can preach from a bucking bronco.

49

- Have the worship leader descend from the ceiling on a cable playing the guitar.[9]

Apparently, some leaders believe that the real presence of Christ needs a little help to draw a crowd. I concur with author John Jefferson Davis, who states that the "church in its worship assemblies needs a fresh manifestation of an *ultimate reality* that can recapture its imagination with a Presence that is more compelling than anything that Spielberg or Pixar Studios can manufacture."[10] Dorothy Sayers puts it most starkly:

> Let us, in heaven's name, drag out the divine drama from under the dreadful accumulation of slipshod thinking and trashy sentiment heaped upon it, and set it on an open stage to startle the world into some sort of vigorous reaction. If the pious are the first to be shocked, so much worse for the pious—others will pass into the kingdom of heaven before them. If all men are offended because of Christ, let them be offended; but where is the sense of their being offended at something that is not Christ and is nothing like him? We do him singularly little honor by watering down his personality till it could not offend a fly. Surely it is not the business of the Church to adapt Christ to men, but to adapt men to Christ.[11]

Jesus Christ is raised from the dead. He is alive! Every Sunday is Easter Sunday because Christ is personally present in the power of the Spirit for and with believers as they worship. This truth is the cosmic game-changer for worship. Our programs and stunts and searches for cutting-edge styles and expensive tech and music equipment can't begin to compete with Jesus among us. Either his presence is enough, or it is not enough. The truth is—it is enough!

Jesus Christ is the central figure of Christian worship. He is the hero of God's story. His person and work is what makes Christian worship *Christian* worship. He is the defining feature that distinguishes our worship from that of any other religion. Ultimately, Christ is God's final word to the world.

Christ is God's final word to the world.

HWJW?

We are now ready to answer the question: How would Jesus worship (HWJW)? Jesus worships God by fulfilling the roles that God gave him: recipient, mediator, leader. He still does. As a human, Jesus worshiped God humbly, taking his place among his followers on earth to join in their worship of the Father. As the divine Son of God, he has also humbly taken his place in heaven to continue his worship of the Father with and for his followers. The worshiped worshiper has and will worship God by accepting the roles given him by God.

HWJW? Jesus worships God by fulfilling the roles God gives him: recipient, mediator, leader.

We too must worship God by accepting our role as humble worshiper. We are human beings with a finite and imperfect capacity to worship God. We bring our worship with honest intentions and sincere hearts. Still, our worship will always stand in need of Jesus's unique assistance that makes it "holy and acceptable to God, which is [our] spiritual worship" (Rom 12:1b NRSV). We must not only accept our limitations as worshipers, but we must also embrace the unique roles that Jesus performs to sanctify our worship, making it worthy to God. There are things that only Christ can do for us; we must eagerly depend upon his services, for right worship depends upon Christ's ongoing ministry.

Do you hear the call—the call of Jesus? "Come follow me…by receiving my priestly assistance that you desperately need in order to join me in worshiping God rightly."

Determining How I Will Worship

Reflection

After looking at Jesus, our role model for worship, it's time to determine what adjustments our Master Teacher may be asking of his disciples. To begin, consider these questions:

- Reflect upon whether or not you are conscious of Jesus's presence in worship. Is it just assumed, taken for granted, or even inadvertently ignored?

- What would it look like for you, as a worshiper, to acknowledge Christ's presence in worship even if your church seemingly overlooks it?

- Think about the three unique roles that Jesus fulfills in our worship—receives, mediates, leads. Which of the three really speaks to you today? Why?

- Try to put in your own words why Christ-centered worship is not in conflict with trinitarian worship. Even though the idea is complex, can you try to explain it in one sentence?

- When you think about Jesus as the true Worship Leader, what excites you the most?

Imagine

It's next Sunday. You walk through the door of the worship space feeling somewhat depleted and possibly even uninterested. You may feel that you do not have the energy to worship God at all. Then you remember that someone else is there to make worship happen—that it doesn't depend entirely on you or the incentive you have at the moment. You remember that Jesus is truly there, offering worship with and for you.

- Identify one specific way that you can intentionally join Jesus in his worship of the Father.

- How can you practice the presence of Christ in worship every Sunday?

Action

With God's help, I determine to focus on the worshiped worshiper by _____. (Be specific.)

Prayer

Risen Lord,

Though you have completed your earthly ministry and have taken your place next to God the Father, I marvel that you are still with us as one of us to make our worship possible. Thank you that your presence is real when your church gathers at all times and places. Fill me with a keen awareness that you are alive and are present to receive our worship, lift it to God, and lead us in proper praise. Because of this, may I rejoice in worshiping you with my brothers and sisters as never before, to the praise of your great Name.

Amen.

Chapter 5

THE DIVINE NARRATIVE OF WORSHIP

KEY QUESTION:
HOW WAS JESUS'S WORSHIP IMMERSED IN THE STORY OF GOD?

Recently a friend told me a beautiful story. It happened that the previous Sunday at his church there was a very special worship service. It was the final service of the Christian year—the Sunday before the season of Advent would begin the annual cycle anew. To help the congregation celebrate the completion of the full story of God in Christ from beginning to end, his pastoral staff devoted the service to a panoramic view of the whole Christian year. They wanted people to remember the grand narrative of God's redeeming work as they prepared to start celebrating it again with the beginning of Advent the following Sunday. Here is my friend's story in his own words.

> Sunday our six-year-old grandson, William, was sitting with my wife, Katie, and me. Usually William is in children's church, but today he chose to sit in "big church" with us. He had declared a few months ago, "I have decided I'm not going to believe anything unless I can see it!" Our conversation went like this:
>
> William: "Is God here?"

Me: "Yes, God is everywhere."

William: "I can't see him."

Me: "Usually we feel God, we don't see God. We can't see God the way we see each other."

William: "I have decided that I won't believe in anything unless I can see it!"

I heard resolve in my grandson's young voice. Even at such a young age I realized that something or someone had intentionally influenced his thinking in that direction. During worship yesterday I looked at William sitting next to me and noticed that he was reading the worship words from the screen and singing along with the songs. He engaged throughout the service as worshipers told the whole story of God. On the short drive home, William said, "When we get home, I need a marker and a new piece of paper." At home, Katie gave him the paper and marker and he disappeared. We started lunch preparations.

Soon William came out with the paper. On it he had written, "I ♥ God!" This didn't come out of Sunday school or children's church, at least not yesterday. This came to him as the church told the dramatic story of God's love in Christ! What a wonderful new statement of belief!

I would add that it wasn't only William's beliefs that were formed. His affections were amended; his love for God was ignited. His church's liturgy was "loaded with an ultimate Story about who we are and what we're for."[1] As a result, William's participation in worship "bent the needle" of his young heart, pointing it to "magnetic north in Christ."[2] He worshiped in the context of the story of God and was moved from skepticism to love.

Describing How We Worship Now

Stories are powerful things. A good story comprises several ongoing narratives that weave together into a masterpiece. Whether in a novel or a nursery rhyme, intriguing characters create plots and subplots as the drama unfolds. Eventually the sequences of events are connected in a way that forms the texture of one great story line. Once connected, the story can then be told because it has a beginning, a middle, and an end.

Listen closely and you will hear that the word *narrative* has crept into our vocabulary almost everywhere on television, on the Internet, and in movies. Athletic coaches speak to athletes about writing a new narrative to inspire better performance; politicians speak of controlling the narrative in order to win elections; attorneys speak of carefully constructing the narrative so as to succeed at trial; a child psychologist helps abused children rewrite their narratives in order to move forward in life. Narratives can be constructive or destructive. Either way, a new reality is formed by whichever narrative is believed. The narrative may or may not even be true or realistic; but it *is* purposeful because in the end it will affect the way a life is lived. We shape our narratives and our narratives shape us.

Our personal story is part of a bigger story whether we realize it or not. It is situated within a "metanarrative," a grand story through which we see the world. (*Meta* means all-encompassing; *narrative* refers to story.) Our stories take place in time and culture, so they make sense only in light of the metanarrative that encompasses them as we connect to the larger world around us. Even though we have our own story, we interpret its meaning through the lens of whatever metanarrative we understand to be true.

God has a story too. We refer to it as the story of God. It is *the* metanarrative of Creation, Incarnation, and Re-Creation. God's story is

the work of the Father, the Son, and the Holy Spirit. God creates, becomes involved with creation, and is made incarnate into time, space, and history in order to redeem and restore the world as the garden of God's habitation and people as his community of love and fellowship.[3]

This great big story of God is told through many biblical narratives weaving their way to a purposeful conclusion. We see the characters and plots, the themes and unfolding drama that adds layer upon layer of texture forming the grand, sweeping story line of reality. At the heart of God's story is God's Son, Jesus the Christ. The story line builds anticipation for his coming, journals his earthly ministry, and describes the future moment "when Christ hands over the kingdom to God the Father" (1 Cor 15:24).

Fortunately, we do not have to create the narrative, for God already has. It is captured in detail in the Old and New Testaments that tell various aspects of this magnificent story over time. Essentially, God's story consists of all that God has done, is doing, and will do.

God's story consists of all that God has done, is doing, and will do.

God's story has a beginning, middle, and end. To say worship *does* God's story is to say that, in worship, we proclaim, celebrate, and enact the story. The story is not only heard; it is actively engaged.

Recently I came across this statement: "If you get the narrative wrong, then you get the solution wrong."[4] The message was clear: the answers aren't going to do you much good if you are already off course with the wrong story line. If we get worship wrong, we get it *all* wrong. So in order to get it right, let's look to our Master Teacher, Jesus, to discover how his worship reflected the story of God.

How was Jesus's worship immersed in the story of God?

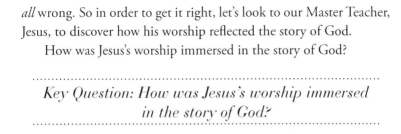

> *Key Question: How was Jesus's worship immersed in the story of God?*

Discovering How Jesus Worshiped

As a Jew, Jesus participated in the public worship that had been instituted by God many centuries before he ever appeared on the world scene. Jesus inherited the faith of his ancestors that shaped his own spiritual story. Historic Hebrew worship was in his DNA. From the very beginning, Jewish worship was entirely identified with God's story—all that God had done, was doing, and would do for his covenant people. By examining Jesus's patterns of worship, we see that he was immersed in God's story in three primary ways: by keeping the Sabbath, by observing the Jewish festivals, and by incorporating the story in the liturgy.

Sabbath as the Story of God

The story of God begins with Creation, and the Sabbath is a huge part of Creation's story. After six days of creation, God rested. In so doing, a seven-day cycle was instituted that included rest for God's creation. For many centuries, observing the Sabbath had mostly to do with ceasing from work so that people, animals, and the land could break from the physical demands of the other six days to be renewed. In the beginning it had little if anything to do with corporate worship, because a permanent place of worship either did not exist or, when it did (much later), it was not accessible to those who lived a distance away from the temple in Jerusalem.[5]

With the giving of the Law, God commanded the people to "re-member the Sabbath day by keeping it holy" (Exod 20:8, NIV). In-terestingly, God's explanation of the commandment mentions rest, but not corporate worship. Resting on the Sabbath *was* the act of worship. But by the time of Jesus, there was a centralized place of worship—the temple; synagogues also existed far and wide. Both places served as sites for Sabbath worship.

The Jews kept Sabbath on Saturday, the seventh day of the week, in commemoration of Creation (though it was marked from sun-down on Friday evening to sundown on Saturday). This 24-hour day was the culmination of the Jewish week. All of the other days moved toward this climax. Time was marked from Sabbath to Sab-bath in one beautiful cycle recalling the seven-day rhythm of God's Creation.

Keeping the Sabbath figured prominently in Jesus's practices of worship. The Gospels are full of examples of Jesus and his disciples worshiping on the Sabbath. It was their pattern. Jesus, along with all devout Jews, kept the Sabbath with rest and worship.

After the resurrection of Jesus, the earliest Jewish disciples began to meet on Sundays as well as the Sabbath as a way of remembering the greatest event in human history, for Sunday was the day of the week when God raised Jesus from death to life. They even named the day of the week "the Lord's Day" as a way of honoring their Lord. Christ's resurrection came to represent the New Creation. This was now the climax of God's story: not Creation—but Re-Creation. As a result, Lord's Day worship for the earliest believers was less about rest but was characterized instead by joyful worship and fellowship.

For many years (no one knows exactly how long), Jewish Christians observed both Saturday worship—by going to temple or synagogue, where they engaged in the liturgies of scriptures and prayers—and Lord's Day gatherings, where they engaged in the lit-urgies surrounding apostolic teaching, prayers, breaking bread, and fellowship. (Both of these scenarios are seen throughout the book of Acts.) Eventually, Christians were no longer welcome at Jewish centers for worship, and it became natural to mark time exclusively by a new cycle: Lord's Day to Lord's Day—Sunday to Sunday. In the fourth century it became official. The Roman emperor Constantine established Sunday as the day of worship for Christians throughout the empire.

By now you might be wondering what keeping the Sabbath has to do with the story of God. A lot, actually. To keep the Sabbath is to enter into the story from the very beginning. The opening scene of humanity's narrative originates with a creating God who established a weekly rhythm inherent in the creation itself by designating one day to keep as holy (Gen 2:2-3). And its purpose is to remember—to remember who God is as the Divine Being seeking relationship with all creation. The keeping of the Sabbath for rest and worship is the primal way to remember that God acts first. To keep the Sabbath is to place your toes on the threshold of the story of God. Before any other chapter of the story unfolds, this holy remembering occurs weekly by God's design. As you keep the designated day of rest and worship, you will begin to cross the threshold and pass through the door to the celebration of the whole story. Gathering to worship every seven days represents the story of God at its core. By keeping the Sabbath, Jesus modeled what it meant to live at the start of the story, beginning with Creation.

Holy Days and Festivals as the Story of God

A second way that Jesus's worship was immersed in the story of God was in his keeping of the Jewish holy days and festivals. Over centuries, the weekly unit of time was expanded into many days and seasons marking how God continued to act in momentous ways for the sake of his people. From Genesis to Revelation, God is seen intervening in human history to fulfill his purposes, and with each demonstration of God's steadfast love, the story of God unfolds chapter by chapter. Jesus was faithful to worship on these holy days and festivals that marked time according to God's story. He participated faithfully and when he did, he was perpetuating the telling of God's story.

The first Jewish festival ever established, Passover, is a prime example. The Passover feast (a set day) and a whole festival of Passover (the week's festivities) recalled God's miraculous acts in delivering his people from centuries of slavery as they marched out of Egypt on dry land through the Red Sea. After a series of devastating plagues, God brought Egypt to its knees by killing the firstborn offspring of people and animals alike. No family was spared except God's people. It was the last straw. Egypt could no longer forbid the Israelites' departure.

The telling of this fantastic story formed the liturgy of the yearly Passover festival. However, the story was told not only with words, but with symbolic reenactment: blood on the doorposts of the Israelites as the sign for God to "pass over" their residences; eating unleavened bread to signal the hurried nature of their exit (yeast had no time to rise); the Passover lamb slaughtered and eaten as a sacrifice to God; eating the meal hurriedly; sandals on their feet and a walking stick in hand in preparation for the journey ahead; and more. The story was told year after year using costumes and props full of rich symbolism.

Passover became the most significant festival of Jewish worship because it was *the* defining narrative in its history. God saw to it that the story would be told to each generation: "You should observe the Festival of Unleavened Bread, because on this precise day I brought you out of the land of Egypt in military formation. You should observe this day in every generation as a regulation for all time" (Exod 12:17). The Exodus event, remembered through the Passover celebration, was the metanarrative through which God's people made sense of all of the narratives of their lives.

All Jewish festivals were occasions for profound worship. Whether solemn or celebrative, the people worshiped their God who delivered them time and again. Numerous holy days and festivals were set apart to commemorate God's provision in dramatic ways by telling and retelling these stories of deliverance from throughout their history, including the Red Sea rescue, the miracle of manna in the wilderness, the conquering of Canaan, bountiful yearly harvests in the land of milk and honey, the preservation of the Jewish race under Queen Esther's leadership, and on the story goes. God established the days and festivals as a way of telling and retelling the metanarrative of his steadfast love.

Jesus is seen observing these holy days and seasons of worship with regularity and great passion. The Gospels specifically mention that he kept the Passover feast (celebrating the escape from Egypt), the Festival of Tabernacles (commemorating God's care in the wilderness with temporary shelters), and the Festival of Dedication (remembering the rededication of the Second Temple in Jerusalem; also known as Hanukkah). If the Jewish calendar called for one of the narratives of God's story to be told, Jesus was there. According to John's Gospel, you couldn't keep him away. It seems that one time Jesus wanted to attend the annual Festival of Tabernacles in Jerusalem, required of all Jewish men. But Jesus told his disciples to go on without him since it was not safe for him to be seen in public. Jewish leaders were looking for their opportunity to kill him. He had a bull's-eye on his back. However, John reports, "after his brothers left for the festival, he went too—not openly but in secret" (John 7:10). Jesus was so impassioned for God's story that he participated even at great risk to his life!

Liturgy and Telling the Story of God

Third, Jesus often told the story of God with painstaking care to his disciples in the context of the liturgy of worship. Jesus frequently tried to explain what God was up to past, present, and future. At his last Passover meal, the night before he was murdered, Jesus rehearsed the story of God to the twelve disciples. He reinterpreted the meaning of the Passover meal in light of his forthcoming betrayal and death, and he spoke of the future kingdom. All of this occurred in the context of the Passover liturgy. (See Matt 26:17-32.) Three nights later, the evening of the Resurrection, he did the same thing. On this occasion Jesus joined two of his disciples on their way home from witnessing the crucifixion. He explained to them the story of God found "in all the scriptures, starting with Moses and going through all the Prophets" (Luke 24:27). The story climaxed with an evening fellowship meal in the disciples' home, where "after he took his seat at the table with them, he took the bread, blessed and broke it, and gave it to them. Their eyes were opened and they recognized him, but he disappeared from their sight" (Luke 24:30-31). Jesus combined a detailed exposition of the story of God with worship at a fellowship meal, which became utterly transformational.

The four Gospels consistently show Jesus to be deeply immersed in the story of God through worship. Christian worship and the story cannot be separated. The story is cause for worship, and worship is cause to celebrate the story. It is a powerful, cyclical, eternal dynamic. God's praise cannot be separated from God's acts. Who God is, is expressed in what God does, for God is a relational Being who reaches out to his creation to compose the story line of history.

Deliberating How Jesus Would Worship Today

Jewish worship of the Old Testament told God's story up to a certain point, but with the coming of the Messiah, the heart of the story is now revealed. Before, worship represented the Old Covenant centered in Abraham; now worship represents the New Covenant centered in Jesus Christ. With the ushering in of the Christian era, we have even more to celebrate when we gather to worship the triune God.

As Christ followers, the very best ways to do God's story is to do what Jesus did: celebrate, reenact, and tell. We participate in the Lord's Day of resurrection as well as the holy days and festivals that testify to God's love and faithfulness over time. For just as the Jews worshiped in remembrance of all that God had done throughout their history as a nation, so Christians also worship in order to remember. We remember all that God has done in Jesus Christ. Christ is the center of God's story because God has made him to "occupy the first place in everything" (Col 1:18). Now holy days find their roots in the life, death, resurrection, ascension, and return of God's Son. Human history forever finds its reference point in Jesus.

Congregations observe an aspect of God's story when they gather to worship on the Lord's Day whether they realize it of not, for the very act of assembling witnesses to the metanarrative in microcosmic form.[6] And most churches tell a part of the story yearly by celebrating Christmas and Easter. But there is so much more to the story! Think about all of the chapters of God's story centered in Christ that include his baptism, his earthly ministry of teaching and miracles, his postresurrection appearances, the coming of the Holy Spirit Jesus promised, the birth of the Church, Christ's return, the judgment, and the creation of a new heaven and a new earth. And this is only the tip of the iceberg.

When worship does God's story, we find ourselves actually observing the Christian year. You may or may not have heard of this term, the *Christian year*. It simply refers to marking time around the metanarrative of God in Christ through the Spirit as we worship. It is to let a "kingdom calendar" reorient our lives to help us put things in perspective. While we all must use a common civil calendar to bring order to our daily lives, as followers of Jesus we are citizens of a heavenly kingdom; earthly time has meaning only in reference to God's larger story. Following the Christian year throughout a calendar year is to worship with the whole story of God over time. It too is a big cycle of fifty-two weeks. Like any great story it is worth repeating. The Christian year is told year after year, not only as a way to remember the story but also to find our place in the story each time. After all, it *is* the greatest story ever told.

Current Challenges

There are many competing metanarratives vying for our acceptance. Each one is impassioned to narrate the world. In fact, this is "the most pressing spiritual issue of our time: *Who gets to narrate the world*."[7] Our answer to that question will have everything to do with how we worship. After all, "how will the world know its own story unless we do that story in public worship?"[8] Today we face some challenges to doing God's story in worship. Two are especially prominent.

My Story or God's Story?

Given our general preoccupation with our own stories (check out your Facebook friends' pages!) and given the diminishing knowledge of God's story, there is concern that "much of our worship has shifted from a focus on God and God's story to a focus on me and my story."[9] We can no longer assume that people have even a basic knowledge of Christianity—as evidenced by a remark my friend overhead by a theatergoer waiting to watch Mel Gibson's *The Passion of the Christ*: "I hear this film is based on a true story."

There is confusion over the relationship between our story and God's story. Robert Webber shares this concern:

> A dominant error of some Christians is to say, "I must bring God into *my* story." The ancient understanding is that God joins the story of humanity to *take us into his story*. There is a world of difference. One is narcissistic; the other is God-oriented. It will change your entire spiritual life when you realize that your life is joined to God's story.[10]

Our stories matter deeply to God, but they are best understood when enfolded into God's cosmic story.

The renowned rabbi Abraham Heschel encountered the same cultural challenge of worshipers contending between God's story and our story. "People complained to him that the synagogue liturgy was not able to say what they meant. 'The goal,' he would respond, 'is not that the liturgy say what you mean but that you mean what the liturgy says.'"[11]

One Narrative or Many Narratives?

Today many people hold the view that there is no such thing as one true metanarrative that governs reality. Instead, they allow for many possible options, any of which are considered to be equally valid. Scripture sets forth a countercultural view, that there is one God with one story centered on one Lord, one faith, and one baptism. Christian worship narrates this story. It is not only our story as believers; it is the story of the world. Worship that is immersed in the divine narrative will help all of us find our place in the story of God. Then we will know that we have gotten the right narrative *and* the right solution.

Who God is and the ways God has worked in salvation history deeply shapes the liturgies of our worship. In short, worship "remembers God's work in the past, anticipates God's rule over all creation, and actualizes both past and future in the present to transform persons, communities, and the world."[12] This is why the story told in worship really matters.

HWJW?

How would Jesus worship if he were here among us today? He would do God's story as the driving narrative of worship.

> *HWJW? Jesus would do God's story as the driving narrative of worship.*

He would celebrate, enact, and tell the story of God. Do you hear the call—the call of Jesus? "Come follow me . . . by stepping into

67

the divine narrative known as God's story and finding your place there."

Determining How I Will Worship

Reflection

After looking at Jesus, our role model for worship, it's time to determine what adjustments our Master Teacher may be asking of his disciples. To begin, consider these questions:

- Is there a family story that is important to your identity? How often do you tell it in family gatherings?

- Reflect upon your seven-day week. Which day seems to be the primary marker? (For instance, Monday to Monday, Friday to Friday, etc.) Why this day?

- Has there ever been a time in your life when you wanted to (or did) rewrite your life's narrative? A time when you determined to take a definitively different path? What made you seek a new driving narrative?

- Do you regularly take advantage of Sabbath rest? Why or why not?

- What do you think is the difference between inviting God into our story or God inviting us into his story?

Imagine

It's next Sunday. You recognize that it is not just the first day of the week on your calendar, but it is actually the Lord's Day. You realize that you are beginning to think of time that is centered on Christ and his kingdom purposes. You imagine yourself among the earliest believers who were excited to gather on Sundays to worship the risen Lord.

- Identify one specific way that you can more intentionally "do God's story" in worship, even if your church isn't driven by the narrative.

- What one concrete action step will you take to become more immersed in the narrative of God?

Suggestion: Even if your church does not observe many of the Christ-events of scripture intentionally over time, try finding some personal devotional material that is formatted around the Christian year. Many people have found that tracing the whole life of Jesus in their daily devotions has deepened their sense of followership, helping them to identify more closely with him.

Action

With God's help, I determine to make worship an occasion for doing God's story by _____. (Be specific.)

Prayer

Thank you, God, for all that you have done, are doing, and will do. Help me to place my story under your story so that I can view the world from within the narrative of your eternal love. Help me to worship you daily in joyous anticipation of the culmination of your grand narrative, when all Creation will join in your ceaseless praise. Through Christ, our Lord. Amen.

Chapter 6

THE CONVERSATION OF WORSHIP

KEY QUESTION:
HOW IMPORTANT WAS DIALOGICAL WORSHIP FOR JESUS?

Good communication is the heart of every significant relationship. You can't really have a relationship without it. So many great things happen when people communicate with each other: we learn about what is important to the other, we speak words of encouragement and comfort, offer praise for a job well done, express our hopes, dreams, concerns and feelings. We also communicate about the everyday details of life—who will walk the dog, take out the trash, mow the lawn, do the laundry? Communication is vital to relationships.

Communication takes lots of different forms. Today we have many devices that help us communicate when not in person. We use cell phones, e-mails, text messaging, video calls, or Facebook, with more technologies developing all the time. Our instant communication capabilities are so amazing that we often expect faster and shorter responses. Abbreviations (LOL) and symbols (emojis) get the job done with little to no conversation. ☺

Even when we are face-to-face, we don't always communicate. I am noticing how many people sit at tables in restaurants using smartphones but not speaking a word to each other until the server brings the meal. They may be communicating with someone, but they are not communicating to the one(s) they are with (unless they are texting each other at the table!). Yes, communication has many forms, but the best is still face-to-face. It captures the sound of the human voice, the expression on the face, the twinkle in the eyes, the hand on the shoulder, the tone of speech.

Made in the image of God, we are relational beings. That is precisely why God engages us in his story, for God's story is a narrative of relationships (see previous chapter). Honest and regular communication is the key to being in any relationship. It's the same for worship.

Describing How We Worship Now

The Christian God is by nature a wholly relational being. Perhaps the most remarkable aspect of Judeo-Christian worship is that God is personally engaged with the community of faith: speaking, listening, intervening, calling, providing for, correcting, guiding, encouraging, and ultimately sending his people to bless the nations. No other god in human history is depicted in such a deeply personal and conversational way. It only makes sense, then, that corporate worship as it developed over time in the Old and New Testaments was dialogical.

Since God is relational in nature, the worship event must be relational in nature, for we must not create a service that is unlike the God we worship. And because worship is relational, it is conversational. Any conversation involves at least two parties to engage in dialogue. A conversation with only one party is a monologue— a conversation with oneself. Biblical worship is dialogical worship. Various worship elements provide avenues of conversation in either direction to support the relationships involved.

In this chapter we will discover the ways in which Jesus practiced the conversational model of worship so that we too enter into dialogue with God and one another.

How important was dialogical worship for Jesus?

Discovering How Jesus Worshiped

To explore Jesus's engagement with dialogical worship, we return to his conversation with the Samaritan woman at Jacob's well. In chapter 3 we found that Jesus worshiped the Father. Jesus clearly established *who* is to be worshiped. Interwoven in that conversation Jesus also speaks to *how* we are to worship the Father: "true worshipers will worship in spirit and truth" (John 4:23). Jesus restated the same phrase to emphasize his point: "God is spirit, and it is necessary to worship God in spirit and truth" (v. 24).

> "...*it is necessary to worship God in spirit and truth.*"
> *(John 4:24)*

It is impossible to separate *whom* one worships and *how* one worships. We must not worship the right God the wrong way. Who is worshiped? The Father. How will true worship take place? In spirit and truth. Here we hit the bull's-eye of what it means to worship from Jesus's point of view. The Father is looking for *true worshipers* (v. 23) who offer *true worship* (v. 24); true worshipers offering true worship do so in spirit and in truth. Anything other than this is false worship, not true worship.

Worshiping in Spirit

To worship in spirit says more about who God is than who we are (yet the two are related). When Jesus told the woman, "God is spirit, and it is necessary to worship God in spirit and truth," he was saying that true worship begins with God and God's nature. The

73

word *spirit* refers to the Holy Spirit of God who generates true worship.[1] Worship is made possible only through the Holy Spirit whom Jesus was about to send to his disciples upon his return to heaven. Some people read verse 24 with a lowercase *s* in mind. Doing so suggests that the key to true worship is the *worshiper's* spirit, assuming that, if they have the proper attitude, they are worshiping in spirit. As important as the posture of the heart is, we are not the starting point for true worship—God is. Of course, because we are created in the image of God, one feature of our multidimensional being is spirit (lowercase *s*). When our natural spirit is born anew (John 3:7), we are joined in fellowship with God for the purpose of worship. Jesus said to the inquisitive Pharisee, Nicodemus, "Whatever is born of the Spirit is spirit" (John 3:6b). True worship is the intersection of God's Spirit with our spirit. However, the emphasis of God *as* spirit is the key to worshiping *in* spirit.[2]

Quite often I will hear someone say that worship should be "authentic." When I ask what is meant, they usually explain that worship is authentic when your heart is right, when you just focus on God, giving yourself with abandon to worship. But notice how authenticity is then defined by the worshiper rather than the One worshiped. God's work and presence is what makes worship authentic. We certainly must participate with the right heart; God warns against improper attitudes. But our attitude is not the standard of measure for whether or not worship is true. Instead, God's incomparable love and self-giving to us in worship is the very definition of authentic worship. "True worship is not what we generate or produce; but true worship is true because it has to do with the One who is himself true—Jesus—with the Spirit of Truth who bears witness to him."[3]

Worshiping in Truth

To worship in truth is to accept the whole revelation of God as given to us in scripture, but most especially as seen in Jesus, who "is the light of God's glory and the imprint of God's being" (Heb

1:3a). Ultimately, truth is a person—the One to whom the scriptures point. Jesus revealed to the woman his identity as Messiah, which is absolutely central to worshiping in truth. Later in the Gospel of John, Jesus makes the bold claim "I am the way, the truth, and the life" (John 14:6a). To worship in truth is to stand in the midst of the story of God (revelation) in order to orient our activity to the Son of God (Revelation).

....
To worship in truth is to stand in the midst of the story of God (revelation) in order to orient our activity to the Son of God (Revelation).
....

Worshiping in truth does not only involve accepting God's revelation intellectually by comprehending a biblical view of worship. It also involves full, vibrant participation in worship with all of one's being—to live into the knowledge of God fully so that the mind is renewed in such a way that we offer ourselves as holy and pleasing sacrifices to God. (See Romans 12:1-2 NRSV.)

Spirit and Truth Are United

Spirit and truth are not two parts of the whole; they are inseparable, as demonstrated by the use of one preposition, *in*, to refer to both dimensions. Some Bible translations include "worship in spirit" and "in truth"; yet the original language uses the preposition only once, signifying that they are organically joined. One cannot worship in spirit without truth, nor in truth without spirit.[4] They are an interdependent dynamic to indicate the wholeness of spiritual worship. It is just not possible to worship in the Holy Spirit without worshiping in the truth as revealed in Jesus Christ, and vice versa.

What does this mean for Jesus's disciples? Jesus teaches us that true worshipers will worship the Father in spirit (they are empowered to worship by the Holy Spirit), and they will worship in truth (their worship conforms to the revealed will of God as seen in scripture).

What's more, spirit and truth are one in purpose and action. But what does this have to do with dialogical worship?

Spirit and Truth Are Dialogical

Worshiping in spirit and truth represents a dialogical relationship that is reciprocal in nature. There is a two-part rhythm that is taking place in worship. We may think of it as a dance between partners. Experienced dance partners don't think so much about what steps they are taking; they simply respond to each other's lead and a dance emerges. The dance is both relational and dialogical. Worshiping in spirit and in truth is both relational and dialogical. One depends on the other.

We see this twofold dynamic often in Jesus the worshiper. Jesus engages in dialogical worship in his primary role as the mediator of worship as we saw in chapter 4. The Incarnate Christ carries the conversation between God and people. In fact, he is the center of the dialogue: *I will publicly announce your name to my brothers and sisters. I will praise you in the middle of the assembly* (Heb 2:12). Jesus both speaks for God in proclaiming God's name to the people, and speaks for the people in leading praise back to God. This role is relational, both vertically and horizontally, and is carried out dialogically.

Jesus also engaged in dialogical worship through his prayers. He prayed in Spirit and in truth. Jesus's life of prayer was very often simply a part of the dialogue of his day-to-day ministry. As such, it was a natural response in the Spirit to the truth of what was being revealed in real time in the lives of his disciples. It was sometimes hard to know where human conversation and God conversation began and ended.

One beautiful example is found in Luke 10:1-24. Jesus sent out seventy-two disciples to announce that God's kingdom had come. They returned joyously to report to the Lord the success of the mission. After giving their full report, "At that very moment, Jesus overflowed with joy from the Holy Spirit and said, 'I praise you, Father,

Lord of heaven and earth, because you've hidden these things from the wise and intelligent and shown them to babies. Indeed, Father, this brings you happiness" (10:21). Jesus's moment of worship (giving praise to the Father), inspired by the Holy Spirit, flowed organically from the truth of the good news he had just heard. Remarkably, as soon as his prayer concluded, he immediately moved back to imparting truth to the disciples: "Turning to the disciples, he said privately, 'Happy are the eyes that see what you see'" (10:23). Jesus worshiped in Spirit and truth by way of natural dialogue in prayer.

There are many other instances of prayerful dialogue in Spirit and truth—occasions when Jesus prayed (led by the Spirit) leading others to conform to the revealed will of God (embracing truth). Dialogical prayer was at the heart of his prayer life because it was based on relationship with God and others. Notice how these few examples demonstrate dialogical prayer:

- Following the final Passover meal, Jesus prayed for future followers: "I'm not asking that you take them out of this world but that you keep them safe from the evil one.... Make them holy in the truth; your word is truth" (John 17:15, 17).

- Jesus alerted Peter, "Satan has asserted the right to sift you all like wheat. However, I have prayed for you that your faith won't fail" (Luke 22:31-32a).

- On the cross Jesus prayed for his murderers: "Father, forgive them, for they don't know what they're doing" (Luke 23:34).

- As he drew his last breath, "Crying out in a loud voice, Jesus said, 'Father, *into your hands I entrust my life*'" (Luke 23:46).

In each of these circumstances and more, Jesus worshiped by praying a Spirit-empowered prayer while at the same time affirming the truth of God's eternal plan. The Spirit helped him stand in the truth of God's revelation; in return, the truth affirmed the Spirit-led prayer. Likewise our lives of worship should represent the union of Spirit and truth.

Deliberating How Jesus Would Worship Today

Dialogical Worship: Revelation and Response

Worshiping in spirit and truth is the foundation of the primary dynamic of worship that is referred to as "revelation and response."

When a community of worshipers gathers before God the conversation naturally unfolds dialogically, the participants speaking in response to each other. In this case, God speaks and listens to the gathered community; we speak and listen to God. This rhythm of interaction resembles Jesus's pattern of worshiping in Spirit and truth. It is also the normative flow of so many of the God-people conversations in scripture.

Revelation and response is the overarching flow of worship. It happens in the large frame of worship—the overall shape of the service. Historically there were four extended movements to worship: the church spent some time gathering in God's presence, heard the scripture read and preached, responded to the word primarily through celebrating the table of the Lord, and then were sent out as empowered citizens of God's kingdom to live the gospel. The word read and preached (revelation) followed by the table of the Lord[5] (response) formed the heart of the dialogue.

At the same time, revelation and response happens throughout the entire service with continuous internal dialogues traveling from beginning to end as they carry out the conversation naturally, much like Jesus's prayers (as seen above). One worship element leads to the next to enable dialogical worship. Recognizing the function of various worship elements can really help us participate better.

Revelation (Worship in Truth)

Revelation refers to the revealed truth that is proclaimed in parts of the conversation, both by God and by the people. Look for declarative statements of the story of God. Here are some worship elements that are common avenues for revelation. (Note: The worship elements listed on the next few pages may or may not be familiar to you, but they represent a wide range of possibilities used by many churches.)

Revelation-Oriented Worship Elements

Scripture Readings	Reading substantial passages as the basis for preaching/teaching
Sermon	Proclaiming the word of God and challenging listeners to live in God's ways
Songs	Proclaiming portions of the story of God
Sacraments/Ordinances	Using words at Holy Communion and baptism that concentrate on God's action
Prayers	Integrating scriptural portions of the story of God within the prayer (examples: praying the Psalms)
Silence	Listening to God speak
Presentational Music	Presenting prepared music to the community that declares portions of the story of God
Sending	Closing words of empowerment to proclaim God's strength and peace

Response (Worship in Spirit)

Response is the reply of God's people to what is revealed. It may be prepared or spontaneous or both. Response elements of worship give the community ways to speak to God in return by acknowledging that we have heard the word and intend to obey God's will as revealed. The "answering" of the community is our response to worship in Spirit. Here are some worship elements that are common avenues for responding to God. (You will notice that some elements overlap because worship elements may serve different purposes.)

Response-Oriented Worship Elements

Scripture Readings	Reading substantial passages as the basis for response such as expressing joy, conviction, surrender, will to obey, etc.
Songs	Responding to the story of God
Sacraments/Ordinances	Using words at Holy Communion and baptism that are in response to God's action
Prayers	Expressing praise, confession, commitment to obey, etc.
Presentational Music	Presenting prepared music to inspire the community in their response to God
Creeds/Affirmations of Faith	Declaring bold statements of Christian belief (examples: "Jesus is Lord!" or the Apostles' Creed)
Tithes/Offerings	Giving God a portion of our income for kingdom purposes
Physical Postures	Kneeling, bowing, prostrating, standing, lifting hands, etc.

Horizontal Dialogue

Revelation and response is not limited exclusively to the vertical direction of worship. Fellow disciples play their part in the conversation with each other too, especially their roles in hospitality, edification, and encouragement. Here are some worship elements that are especially well suited for horizontal flow.

Horizontally Directed Worship Elements

Greeting/Welcome	Using words and gestures to extend hospitality to each worshiper
Passing of the Peace	Affirming that we share the peace of Jesus Christ, thereby expressing reconciliation and oneness (example: "The Peace of Christ be with you" and the response, "And also with you")
Songs	Encouraging other worshipers
Intercessions	Praying on behalf of others (examples: prayers for healing, comfort, persons in prison, persecuted Christians, those holding civil office, countries at war, etc.)
Petitions	Praying on behalf of self and fellow believers (example: ministries of the local church, church staff, outreach initiatives, etc.)
The Lord's Prayer	Connecting Jesus's followers in prayer worldwide
Testimonies	Witnessing to fellow worshipers as to how we have experienced God at work in our lives
Exhortation	Encouraging believers to grow in faith, trust, and obedience
Washing Feet	Stooping to serve others in a most humbling symbolic act of Christian love
Anointing with Oil	Using a biblical symbol of healing and shalom when praying for healing of all types of brokenness
Benedictions	Blessing one another with words of peace, promise, and assurance

Thus far we have seen that the pattern of revelation/response represents a dialogical model for corporate worship consisting of both vertical and horizontal movement. The flow of the conversation is

VERTICAL

HORIZONTAL

not prescribed; it moves freely between parties, just like talking to a friend.

That being said, it is very important that the worship conversation starts in the right place. Biblical worship begins with revelation, not response. This is because God is the God who initiates relationship. Look carefully at the many God-human conversations in scripture and you will see that God makes the first move toward people. God calls, God comes, God speaks, God approaches *first*. It is to the gracious initiatives of God that worshipers respond. That's why very often a service begins with a God-focused call to worship or greeting or prayer that establishes God's role in reaching out to the community. Again, our services must reflect the God we worship. Two problems emerge if we begin with human response: (1) worship becomes immediately focused on us before God, and (2) the one to whom we are responding is not yet established. Neither one is a good starting place. God initiates the conversation that unfolds with revelation and response.

Current Challenges

Sometimes the pattern of revelation and response can accidentally be overshadowed, challenging the dialogical nature of worship.

One current challenge is self-focused worship—worship that starts and ends with us. A few years ago I received a phone call from Jonathan. Jonathan was the worship pastor at a large, multisite church. He was attempting to provide his young worship leaders at the various sites with training in order to help them mature in leadership. He arranged for a conference call between his leaders and me to talk about some of the things they were learning.

In the course of the conversation I learned that one of their areas of growth was the discovery that God initiates worship. Frankly, they said, "Until recently we had never thought about the fact that God initiates worship." When I inquired as to how that new insight had influenced how they now lead worship, they responded, "We used to start each service about us. Now we make it clear that we are there to respond to God's invitation to worship. The tone of the service has shifted. The center of gravity moved from us to God. It has made all of the difference in the world!"

A second contemporary challenge is imbalance between revelation and response. Some churches lean heavily upon information-driven sermons (revelation). Preaching can dominate the service with virtually no attention given to responding to the word. Other churches emphasize lengthy times of expressive worship, especially in extended times of response-oriented singing. While the sermon may be important, singing is referred to as "worship" and takes priority. Occasionally the sermon is shortened or even eliminated altogether when the singing dominates. In either scenario, dialogical worship is diminished.

A third challenge is to understand that dialogue does not depend entirely on words. Think about how many times when, with friends and family, your conversation occurs through nonverbal communication. The arts play a vital role in dialogical worship—the fine arts, visual arts, movement arts, the use of symbols and colors, and so forth. Too often we have leaned almost exclusively on the musical arts or spoken art forms to carry the dialogue. Yet often, profound things are communicated without a word ever spoken. We should not underestimate how powerful the nonverbal art forms of communication can be in contributing to revelation and response.

HWJW?

How would Jesus worship if he were here among us today? He would fully engage in dialogical worship to inspire worship in Spirit and truth. He would pursue relational worship based on conversation as a means for connecting with God and others. Do you hear the call—the call of Jesus? "Come follow me...by worshiping God in Spirit and in truth."

HWJW? He would fully engage in dialogical worship to inspire worship in Spirit and truth.

Determining How I Will Worship

Reflection

After looking at Jesus, our role model for worship, it's time to determine what adjustments our Master Teacher may be asking of his disciples. To begin, think about these questions:

- Who is the person in your life with whom it is the easiest to converse? Why do you suppose it is so easy?

- Which do you count on the most for effective worship— you having the right spirit (frame of mind) or the Holy Spirit? Explain.

- What does "authentic worship" mean to you?

- In your own experience, has there been one side of worship, revelation or response, that seems more important? If so, why?

- In your daily life, do you move freely in dialogical prayer, going back and forth between speaking to people and speaking to God? How could you foster this type of worship?

- Looking at the three separate lists of worship elements found in this chapter, find one that seems unfamiliar to you. How might it help you in dialogical worship?

Imagine

It's next Sunday. As you prepare for worship, imagine that you are sitting at Jacob's well along with the Samaritan woman and Jesus. You hear him say, "True worshipers worship in Spirit and truth. The Father looks for those who worship him this way." You suddenly find yourself with a heartfelt desire to be one of the true worshipers Jesus is talking about. For the first time in a long while, you don't want to be preoccupied with certain external features of worship. Instead, your prayer is to focus on authentic (true) worship.

- Identify some specific ways that that you may more deeply embrace worship in Spirit and truth.

- What one concrete action step will you take to move toward becoming a true worshiper?

Action

With God's help, I determine to _____ by _____. (Be specific.)

Prayer

Jesus, my Master,

As your follower, I long to understand what it means to be a true worshiper, the kind of worshiper the Father seeks. Send the Holy Spirit to lead me to worship in Spirit and truth. Help me to pursue true worship now and always. Thank you, God, for being a relational God in Three Persons who reaches out to us first and invites us into the dialogue of worship. Help us all to respond in joyful worship to the praise of your glory.

Amen.

Chapter 7

THE DISCIPLE AS PARTICIPANT OF WORSHIP

KEY QUESTION:
WHAT QUALITIES DID JESUS EXHIBIT AS A WORSHIPER?

C hances are you've applied for a job at some point in your life. When you did, an application was involved. Perhaps it was a written application followed by a face-to-face interview. You likely had to supply names of references that could verify you had the very qualifications the employer was looking for. Or maybe the "application" was more of an informal, verbal explanation of what the job entailed with the promise of on-the-job training. If you were willing to give it a try, you were hired with just a handshake. Either way, every job opening sets forth certain qualifications that are needed for the position.

One time I applied for a job and the potential employer turned the tables in the interview. I was asked, "What makes for a good employee?" It took me off guard. What *does* make for a good employee? My qualifications were evident in the application in front of him; however, he was interested not only in my skill and experience, but my character and attitude as well. What personal qualifications would I bring to the job?

Before you read this chapter, take a moment to create a list of all of the qualities that you think make for a good worshiper. Keep this list handy for later reference.

This chapter is about the individual participant of worship; the next chapter discusses the community of worship participants.

Describing How We Worship Now

What Makes for a Good Worshiper?

Prior to composing your list, had you ever thought about what makes for a good worshiper? Often we think about what we hope to get out of worship. But what do we plan to give as a worshiper? So I wonder: What expectations does God have for worshipers? What virtues are helpful? It's a popular sentiment today that you can come as you are to worship; yet that is only partially true. While God understands where we are at any point in our spiritual journey, it is not true that God is pleased with any manner with which we choose to present ourselves for worship.

Both the Old and New Testaments emphasize the necessity of right preparation for worship. Before the Israelites could enter the tabernacle or temple area, certain purification rites were required (Ps 24:3-5); Paul addressed New Testament believers concerning how to prepare themselves for worship by solving divisions before participating in the table of the Lord (see 1 Cor 11–14); and James advised the early Christians to abolish favoritism between the rich and the poor prior to worship (Jas 2:1-13). There are actually many admonitions in the scriptures urging God's people to give attention to the manner in which they come to worship.

In worship, we both receive and give. Christian worship promises a great deal to those who actively engage in it with the right spirit. Consider what we receive in corporate worship:

- communion with the triune God
- spiritual fellowship with other believers
- encouragement in our Christian faith
- forgiveness of sin
- enlightenment from the scriptures
- nourishment at the table to live the holy life
- empowerment from the Holy Spirit for doing mission
- spiritual transformation (both personal and corporate)

God gives the gift of worship to his people. And what a gift it is!

However, like anything, what we get out of it depends largely upon what we put into it. Imagine, for a moment, that God has turned the tables. Instead of asking you what you want from worship, God interviews *you*, asking you what qualities you are willing to develop in order to approach worship with right attitudes and right engagement. There is no better place to go for discovering what makes for a faithful worshiper than to look to Jesus, our worship mentor, to examine his attitude and engagement as a worshiper.

What qualities did Jesus exhibit as a worshiper?

Key Question: What qualities did Jesus exhibit as a worshiper?

Discovering How Jesus Worshiped

The Gospels portray Jesus as a remarkable worshiper. Of course! He was divine. The qualities Jesus demonstrates may be placed in two categories: proper faith and proper means.

Chapter 7

Proper Faith

Jesus's qualifications as a faithful worshiper begin with his own personal faith. Yes, Jesus possessed deep personal faith—a faith that he inherited from his parents and the greater Jewish tradition in which he was steeped. At the same time, his faith clearly became his own as he grew into adulthood. All occasions of Jesus's worship are rooted in his identity as a believer in God and as a member of his faith community.

Jesus was identified as a member of the household of God from infancy. Luke situates Jesus's birth in the context of the Jewish community with its lawful expectations. On the eighth day following his birth, he was circumcised and received the name Jesus, given to Mary earlier by the angel (Luke 2:21). His circumcision officially placed him directly within the household of faith. On the heels of this event, Joseph and Mary took him to the temple to fulfill Mary's purification rites. There they offered the proper animal sacrifice to redeem their firstborn son, according to the Law of Moses[1] (Luke 2:22-24). Luke presents Joseph and Mary as very devout worshipers, intent upon fulfilling every requirement of the Law (Luke 2:39). Only after doing so did they leave Bethlehem to return to their home in Nazareth.

As time went on, Jesus demonstrated a developing interest in his faith. A classic example is seen in the story of his adventure in the temple during the family's annual Passover trip to Jerusalem. (See Luke 2:41-52.) One year the boy Jesus took full advantage of the opportunity to take his faith to the next level. For days he sat among the religious teachers within the temple compound where rabbinic instruction took place. There, Jesus listened to their teaching and asked them questions; in return, the rabbis would pose counter questions for the student to answer. This methodology for religious education was very common in Jewish culture and helps to explain Luke's report: "Everyone who heard him was amazed by his understanding and his answers" (Luke 2:47).

We see how significant it was to Jesus to be at the temple. When his parents reprimanded him for staying behind when their caravan had left the city, the boy, no doubt in wonderment, replied, "Why were you looking for me? Didn't you know that it was necessary for me to be in my Father's house?" (Luke 2:49).

This chapter in Jesus's faith development gives us a window into his growing personal faith. He longed for spiritual understanding; he found being in God's house a necessity. Luke affirms the qualities found in Jesus, the maturing worshiper: "The child grew up and became strong. He was filled with wisdom, and God's favor was on him" (Luke 2:40).

The initial quality Jesus brought to his life of worship was personal faith. In adulthood his faith continued to be nurtured through spiritual disciplines such as prayer, fasting, meditation, and solitude. Relationship with God is a prerequisite for true worship.

Proper Means

Throughout Jesus's adult life as a worshiper, he embodied the essence of his ancient faith tradition. The core of his Jewish faith was found in its succinct summary known as the *Shema*,[2] a creedal statement given by Moses to the Israelites just prior to their inheriting the land God promised: "Hear, O Israel: The LORD is our God, the LORD alone. You shall love the LORD your God with all your heart, and with all your soul, and with all your might" (Deut 6:4-5 NRSV). First is the statement of faith: the Lord alone is our God. This is followed by the appropriate intentions: therefore we must love our God with all our heart, soul, and might. This is a beautiful example of revelation/response, so indicative of relational faith found throughout the scriptures.

Jesus publicly endorsed this statement of faith, referring to it as the Great Commandment.[3] More important, in worship he expressed his love for God with all of his heart, soul, mind, and strength (Mark 12:30).[4] It can be tempting to think of these four words as separate

91

ways of loving God; but that is to misunderstand the ancient Hebrew view. They simply can't be separated because in Hebrew, they
hold much more of an integrated sensibility. To a degree, the terms
are interchangeable. Each one has its own sweet spot, yet each one
also refers to some or all of the other dimensions too.

Each of these ways of loving God represents a domain, yet none
of them acts independently from the others. To operate in one domain is to operate in all of them at once. It's like playing basketball.
At any given point in a game, a player may concentrate on dribbling,
or footwork, or blocking shots, or passing the ball; yet, even though
one may be highlighted, all of the skills are working in concert with
one another at the same time.

If we think of these aspects only as separate means for worshiping God, we will have missed the main point. They do not form a
list whereby it would be possible to engage in some but not others.
All of these dimensions together are what the scriptures intend as necessary for worship. The ancient understanding of the command to love
God with our heart, soul, mind, and strength is to love God with all
of our being—with everything that we are, with everything that we
have. The Oneness of God (in the first phrase of the *Shema*) is followed by the oneness of intentions (in the second part).

Still, in the Gospels we are given snapshots of Jesus worshiping
that seem to highlight loving God in specific ways. As we turn to
these now, keep in mind the big picture of which these accounts are
only a part—that while each one simply gives us a glimpse of a moment in time, Jesus worshiped with all of his being, with all that he
had, all of the time.

Jesus worshiped with all of his heart (affective engagement). Jesus
expressed emotion in worship. One example may surprise you. One
day, while in the temple, Jesus discovered that merchants were sell-
ing animals needed for sacrifices. What's more, they presumably were
doing so for unethical gain, taking advantage of the people. This en-
raged Jesus, who unleashed his anger by making a whip from nearby
ropes, chasing the sellers and animals out of the temple, upsetting

the tables, and spilling the coins from the cash registers. Jesus's raw emotions were on display that day. His words were forceful: "It's written, *My house will be called a house of prayer*. But you've made it a hideout for crooks" (Matt 21:13). His disciples, noting his fury, understood it in retrospect when they "remembered that it is written, *Passion for your house consumes me*" (John 2:17, referencing Ps 69).

On another occasion, in a moment of public prayer at the death of Lazarus, Jesus wept in sympathy with others and out of his own personal sorrow (John 11:33-36). He was "deeply disturbed" as he began his prayer for Lazarus to be raised from death (11:38, 41-44). Jesus freely expressed emotion in worship. He demonstrated that to feel is part of what it means to be human.

Jesus worshiped with all of his soul (whole-being engagement). His faithful participation at synagogue and temple demonstrate Jesus worshiping with all of his soul. Synagogues were places of worship involving whole-being involvement: creedal confessions of faith, the recitation of the *Shema*, prayers, scripture readings, interpretation of the readings, and discussion led by qualified participants.[5] The first chapter of Mark includes Jesus's participation at synagogue as one of the earliest events reported. Right after his baptism, Jesus called his disciples and then went to synagogue! It was his routine to go to synagogue on the Sabbath day. Jesus was equally committed to worship in the temple. The four Gospels abound with references to Jesus worshiping regularly in the synagogue and the temple, places where worshipers' whole being was engaged.

Jesus worshiped God with all of his mind (rational engagement). Jesus engaged his mind in worship. He did so primarily as a teacher. Jesus's teaching ministry predominates throughout the stories in the Gospels. In multiple settings—on the hillside, in homes, walking from place to place, from a boat—wherever Jesus was, he taught. Most of all, he taught daily in the temple. (See Matt 26:55; Mark 14:49; Luke 22:53.) As we have seen, Jesus also participated as a reader of scripture in the synagogue. Not only did he read, he offered commentary upon it. (See Luke 4:16-21.) He participated in a multidimensional ministry of teaching, reading, prophetic commentary, and exhortation, all of which engaged his mind as a worshiper.

Jesus did not just have knowledge; he demonstrated phenomenal moral and spiritual understanding. All who heard him "were amazed at the gracious words that came from his mouth" (Luke 4:22 NRSV). Worshiping with all your mind also includes moral and spiritual understanding. From Jesus's point of view, information results in formation.

Jesus worshiped God with all of his might (physical engagement). Worshiping with all of one's might involves many dimensions such as physical, economic, and social strength.[6] Jesus was limited in his economic and social standing, yet he worshiped God with full physical abandon. He knelt, bowed, stood, touched, raised hands, raised his face to heaven, ate at ritual feasts, gave offerings, and more. Worship is very tactile, engaging all of the human senses of sight, sound, smell, taste, and touch.

Jesus gave so much of himself in worship that there were occasions when he needed supernatural strength to fulfill his desire to be a faithful worshiper. God provided it. Angels were sent to take care of Jesus to replenish his strength when he found himself depleted from his spiritual contest with the devil (Matt 4:11). Jesus knew that to love the Lord his God with all his might could be a great battle of the flesh. He said so to his disciples on an occasion when he was struggling in prayer at the end of his earthly ministry: "The spirit is eager, but the flesh is weak" (Matt 26:41). On this occasion, too, a heavenly angel came to strengthen him while he knelt in prayer (Luke 22:43).

The use of our bodies plays a significant part in biblical worship. We employ them to bow, kneel, stand, embrace, dance, raise hands, lift heads, clap, shout, and much more. Biblical worship can be a workout! Yet to worship with all of our might is more than undertaking physical activity; it goes beyond particular actions to include worshiping with all of the fortitude God provides through the Spirit for energetic worship. Strength to worship God is a gift from God.

We do not worship in our own power, but God provides all that is needed to be a faithful worshiper. If we truly desire to worship God with all our might, we will often experience heavenly help to do just that.

In addition to Jesus's demonstration of loving God wholly, he also taught his disciples concerning specific virtues needed for worship. Here are some of them:

- humility (don't pray for show like hypocrites)
- self-control (don't babble on when you pray)
- persistence (keep on asking, seeking, knocking)
- respect for historic faith (requiring those healed to make the proper sacrifices according to Moses's Law)
- proper perspective (the spirit of the Law supersedes the traditions of the Law)
- disdain for legalism (the Pharisees tithed to the extreme but neglected people)
- resistance to empty ceremony (don't fast in public to be noticed)
- reverence (cleansing the temple from money changers)
- reconciliation (making things right with your brother or sister before presenting your gift at the altar)
- self-sacrificial worship (the poor widow praised whose offering was everything she had to live on)
- zeal (consumed with passion for God's house)
- worship in spirit and truth (both proper means and proper faith)
- love supersedes sacrifices (God wants mercy above sacrifice)
- authenticity (not honoring God with our lips while our hearts are far from God)

- inclusive worship (do not consider wealth or social standing in worship)
- hospitality (Jesus welcomed the little children into his arms)

What if this list of proper means became our list of the qualities we seek to worship God?

Deliberating How Jesus Would Worship Today

Jesus has shown us what it means to be a faithful worshiper by modeling proper faith and proper means.

Proper Faith in Worship Today

The first qualification for a faithful worshiper is that she or he is a Christian. Personal, saving faith in Jesus Christ is the number one qualification for Christian worship. Theologians refer to the relationship between faith and worship by using the terms *orthopraxy* and *orthodoxy*. (*Ortho-* means right or correct, *-praxy* refers to faith, and *-doxy* has to do with praise.) The proposal is this: right faith (orthopraxy) is necessary for right praise (orthodoxy). At the same time, right praise—worshiping in spirit and in

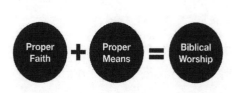

truth—forms us in right faith. Right praise and right faith work interdependently. You can't have one without the other, like so many of the themes we have mentioned in this book. Nevertheless, right worship begins with right belief.

Here we must note a couple of very important things. First, claiming genuine faith in God through Jesus Christ as a necessity for true worship does not, of course, preclude the worship of young children who are growing into faith, who are learning to worship God as the community is forming them in praise. Jesus affirms the sheer delight of the little ones offering their hosannas to the Son of David. He turns their praise back to God: "Out of the mouths of infants and nursing babies you have prepared praise for yourself" (Matt 21:16, NRSV; see Ps 8:2).

Neither does it suggest that people may not worship God according to the degree of knowledge available to them. The scripture speaks of all people having a consciousness that creation exhibits God's invisible qualities and divine nature (Rom 1:20; Ps 8:1-9). In that sense they may have a vague awareness that there is a God and may even desire to worship this God, doing so according to their degree of knowledge to which they are accountable (Rom 2:14-16).

Special considerations aside, the principle remains: true worship is based on Jesus Christ, the Revelation of God, who is the pathway to true worship. "In the past, God spoke through the prophets to our ancestors in many times and many ways. In these final days, though, he spoke to us through a Son" (Heb 1:1-2a). We must come to worship placing our trust in the one who announced to the Samaritan woman, "I AM" (the Messiah). (See John 4:25-26.) Right faith is necessary for right worship.

Proper Means for Worship Today

God has established certain expectations for the Christian community as it gathers in his presence. There are clues throughout the scriptures. The means include such things as confession (James 5:16), reverence and awe (Heb 12:28), orderly manner (1 Cor 14:40), interdependence of Christian sisters and brothers (1 Cor 14:26), joyfulness (Ps 100:2), and our whole being (Ps 103:1).

It's very important to realize that the way in which we live out God's expectations for worship will vary greatly from culture to culture. There is no one-and-only way to approach worship. We must seek to start with God's standards and then engage them faithfully in an appropriate manner from within our native cultures. Worship will (and must) look different from place to place in our world, even within a given country. The thing to keep in mind is that God sets the standard, not culture. There are ways to conform to God's expectations for worship *and* do so in a way that is meaningful to any group of people.

It is our joy to seek out God's plans for worship and make them our lifelong pursuit. In this way we bring pleasure to God, while we receive an experience of deeply satisfying worship in return.

Current Challenges

Our desire is to be discipled in the ways and means of worship that resemble Jesus's worship of God. As his disciples, we will need to be aware of a few challenges to his example of proper faith and proper means that have emerged in recent years.

✝ THE PROPER FAITH CHALLENGE

One current challenge is the assumption that you do not have to be a Christian to worship God. It is quite popular in some circles to gear worship services toward unbelievers, even to create services for that exclusive purpose. Yet to do so is to fundamentally misunderstand the role of faith in worship.

Christian worship has to do both with *Christology* (a keen understanding of Christ's role in worship) and *ecclesiology* (a keen understanding of the church). The church consists entirely of Christ-followers who name Jesus as Lord and follow him as their Head.

Christian worship is the primary means through which the church is the church. I am not speaking of the church as a building. Rather, the church on earth is the visible reality of the invisible, eternal kingdom of God. And both the church and the kingdom of God comprise all those who profess the lordship of Jesus Christ. For Christians, therefore, worship services are a means to profoundly realize their corporate fellowship with God and one another in order to *be* the church on earth. In essence, "the nature of the church cannot be understood apart from its calling as a worshiping community. It is through worship that the church is decisively shaped *as* the ecclesial community."[7]

We are hard-pressed to find any example in scripture or the early church to affirm that corporate worship was for unbelievers. In fact, we find the opposite. The unbeliever's understanding is described as being veiled until Christ removes the veil (2 Cor 3:14). Paul explains why this veil is there: "The god of this age has blinded the minds of those who don't have faith so they couldn't see the light of the gospel that reveals Christ's glory" (2 Cor 4:4). We cannot worship God acceptably without the spiritual transformation God gives. Faith in Christ is required not only for worship on earth but also for worship in heaven. The great crowd of worshipers from every nation, tribe, people, and language who stand before the throne and before the Lamb are those who have overcome great hardship and are clothed with white robes washed in the Lamb's blood (Rev 7:9-14). "This is the reason they are before God's throne. They worship him day and night" (Rev 7:15).

During the opening centuries of Christendom, early church leaders were insistent that nonbelievers could not engage in some aspects of worship. Welcomed, yes; able to comprehend and participate in all aspects, no. *Seekers* (that very term was used) were on a path toward faith involving several stages; but until they were converted, they were dismissed after the sermon and not permitted to proceed to the Table (Holy Communion). They were not even permitted to pray the Lord's Prayer.[8] Once converted, signified in baptism, they were no longer seekers but "faithful." Part of the conversion ceremony required the seeker to renounce "all association with pagan ideologies and habits and commit solely to the worship of the triune God."[9] Another part of the liturgy involved renouncing non-Christian worship while the candidate proclaimed allegiance to Jesus Christ.[10]

Today if you travel in various places in Europe, you can see baptisteries next to churches. Separate physical structures were erected so that nonbelievers could publicly declare their faith through baptism prior to entering the church as a full participant in worship. This ancient practice is a picture of the commitment to proper faith united with proper means for worship.

In our Christian culture today, we should certainly not exclude unbelievers from worship. It is urgent that they are invited and warmly embraced. Yet neither should we hijack the biblical understanding of worship in order to alter its purpose based on some mistaken idea that worship is for non-Christians. Evangelism is not the purpose of corporate worship; the purpose of worship is for God to meet with the assembly of believers to foster relationship through God's revelation and our response. "*Worship is never meant to serve any other purpose except the glory of God.* The end of worship is worship."[11]

Here is where it gets exciting. Nothing is so powerful, evangelistically speaking, as the unbeliever witnessing Christ-followers meeting with God in true devotion. Paul describes this scenario when addressing the Corinthian church at worship. He indicates that if "an unbeliever or outsider comes in" while you are worshiping *properly* (that is his point), they are convicted (1 Cor 14:24). Then "the secrets of their hearts are brought to light. When that happens, they will fall on their faces and worship God, proclaiming out loud that truly God is among you!" (1 Cor 14:25). Good worshipers produce good worshipers! Right faith is necessary for right worship; and the result reaches beyond the circle of believers to profoundly affect unbelievers. Harold Best says it so well: "Christian witness is overheard worship."[12] Are you interested in evangelizing the lost? Try bringing worship to increasing conformity with God's purposes, and then get ready to celebrate conversions.

✝ THE PROPER MEANS CHALLENGE

As we have seen, even as Jesus demonstrated proper faith, he demonstrated proper means as a worshiper. *How* we worship is very important. The qualities we bring to worship matter.

A second current challenge to becoming a faithful worshiper is the widespread opinion that we can make worship into whatever we want it to be. But notice that when we do this, *we* become the standard for worship. We presume that if it is acceptable to us, it is acceptable to God. Again, quite the opposite is true. We should not decide what we want out of worship and then line everything up to our satisfaction. We should not set forth what we want to do and then ask God to come on board.

At first, Psalm 51 seems to suggest that the means (sacrifices and burnt offerings) are unimportant: "For you [Lord] have no delight in sacrifice; if I were to give a burnt offering, you would not be pleased. The sacrifice acceptable to God is a broken spirit; a broken and contrite heart, O God, you will not despise" (Ps 51:16-17, NRSV). But read further. After the worshiper's heart is right, "then you will delight in right sacrifices, in burnt offerings and whole burnt offerings; then bulls will be offered on your altar (v. 19). Throughout scripture we see the importance of having the right heart (pure intentions, humble spirit, etc.) to be a good worshiper. Yet however necessary such qualities are, they do not exclude the God-ordained means for worship. A heart of worship *plus* the fulfillment of the requirements for worship are both needed. One without the other is unbiblical worship.

We have come full circle back to the *Shema*. We are ready to join Jesus by worshiping with everything we have, with everything we are! We follow his lead by loving God with all our heart, soul, mind, and strength.

101

HWJW?

We are now ready to answer the question: How would Jesus worship (HWJW)? Jesus would worship out of his deep, personal faith in God, and he would do so with his whole being—with everything he had! He would worship God with proper faith and through proper means.

> *HWJW? Jesus would worship God with proper faith and through proper means.*

We too must follow Jesus in worship through proper faith and through proper means. Becoming a faithful worshiper is a process because discipleship is a process. Be patient with yourself as you pursue right faith united with right means. However, if you engage in this pursuit for a lifetime, your worship will never be the same.

Do you hear the call—the call of Jesus? "Come follow me...by loving the Lord your God with all your heart, soul, mind, and strength."

Determining How I Will Worship

Reflection

After looking at Jesus, our role model for worship, it's time to determine what adjustments our Master Teacher may be asking of his disciples. To begin, go back to the list you created of good qualities for worshipers earlier in this chapter. Take a few moments to make any adjustments you wish as a result of what you have learned. Are there any qualities that you would add or take away? If so, why are you interested in making these changes?

Now take another step. Ask: Which characteristics of the faithful worshiper are your strongest? Which qualities could you work on? Share your intentions with a fellow worshiper to encourage each other in your pursuit of worship discipleship.

Imagine

It's next Sunday. On your way to church you catch yourself looking forward to how much you will get out of worship. Then you remember that there is something to give as well. You are encouraged that you will be worshiping out of your personal relationship with God in Jesus Christ. Then:

- review some of the qualities that make for a good worshiper from God's point of view;

- offer a prayer that God's Spirit will help you to enter into worship with the proper attitudes and intentions;

- ask for supernatural strength to love the Lord your God with all your heart, soul, mind, and strength.

Later on in the day you discover that your prayers were answered and that it changed everything.

Action

Now set your goal for becoming a faithful worshiper by completing this sentence:

With God's help, I determine to _____ by _____.
(Be specific.)

Prayer

Dear God,

I long to worship you with all of my being—heart, soul, mind, and strength. Send your Holy Spirit to strengthen me to engage in God-pleasing worship through Jesus Christ, my Lord. May my faith become more vibrant and my worship a great witness to the beauty and power of life lived in the presence of the Risen Lord! May others see this and desire it too. I pray this for the sake of the world and the glory of your name. Amen.

Chapter 8

THE COMMUNITY OF WORSHIP

KEY QUESTION:
HOW DID JESUS PARTICIPATE IN COMMUNAL WORSHIP?

I prefer to worship on my own. I've heard this statement many times. Perhaps you have too. John was an introvert who felt unsettled when asked to participate in worship. Linda was a corporate executive who preferred worshiping out on the water in her boat on her only day off. Alex had a rotating schedule in the factory and was just plain tired on Sundays. Abbey was a teenager who stayed up late on Saturday nights to go out with her friends. Ted thought the church was full of hypocrites and preferred to avoid them. Each one chose to go solo when it came to worship.

Most folks in the Western world have the option of participating in a weekly Christian worship service. If they opt for private worship over corporate worship due to personal preference, have they made their decision based on two equal options? In other words, is worshiping on your own the same as worshiping with other persons of faith? There are people who simply cannot join others to worship God due to real circumstances that restrict their ability to come to church. This is understandable. But the question remains, why choose to join with other persons to worship in community when you can worship on your own?

It's a wonderful thing to have private times of worship with God. The Bible is full of examples of individuals offering worship on their own: Abel offered an acceptable sacrifice from his flock (Gen 4:4), Jacob built an altar after wrestling with the angel of the Lord (Gen 28:16-18), Hannah presented herself before the Lord at the temple (1 Sam 1:9-11), and John the Baptist had long periods of solitude in the desert, to name a few. At one level, worship is always personal in that each of us is in relationship with God on the basis of our faith in Jesus Christ. Naturally, then, there are times of worship that are meant to be intimate moments between God and us. We have these moments when we have our daily devotions, when we go on a personal retreat, or when we practice the moment-by-moment awareness of God's presence throughout our day.

Yet while private worship is one important dimension of nurturing our relationship with God, it is only part of the worship experience; God has something more than private worship in mind. God's plan is for individual believers to physically gather as the body of Christ to offer corporate devotion to God and be formed by the Spirit in the process. Worship was designed to be corporate at its core. Biblical worship is worship done in community.

Describing How We Worship Now

Something very different happens when worshipers assemble for public, rather than private, occasions of worship. Worship is the unique and essential gathering of God's people as a local body of Christian disciples who express acts of corporate devotion to the triune God in partnership with one another. Two complementary words are helpful in understanding the beauty and power of God's people gathering together for worship.

First is the English word *corporate*, based on the Latin word *corpus,* referring to the human body. Paul uses the metaphor of the body to paint a picture of the church: "A body is a unit and has many parts; and all the parts of the body are one body, even though there are many.... You are the body of Christ and parts of each other" (1 Cor 12:12, 27). In corporate worship, all parts of the body engage at a high level of functionality so that each one contributes to the beautiful endeavor of adoring God. Corporate worship depends upon the contributions of each member of the family of God as together we offer our gifts for the good of the whole. That's what Paul had in mind when he challenged a local congregation, "When you meet together [in worship], each one has a psalm, a teaching, a revelation, a tongue, or an interpretation. All these things must be done to build up the church" (1 Cor 14:26). Corporate worship is a group effort as each worshiper contributes her or his part. Worship is a team sport!

The second word is *communal*, related to similar words like *communion* and *community*. Communal worship takes corporate worship to a deeper level. Communal worship is less about functionality and more about fellowship. The New Testament Greek word *koinonia* is translated as both "fellowship" and "communion," speaking of the relationship of believer-to-believer. It is also translated as "participation," but participation at a very deep level—not just engaging in common activity but more in the shared experience of love for Jesus Christ and one another. Communal worship is to offer ourselves without reservation so as to experience union with Christ and also with our brothers and sisters. In communal worship we are drawn into an incredible depth of fellowship that results from full, Spirit-filled engagement. Christian community isn't something we create; it is a gift from God that is a reality by virtue of being made one in Christ. It is discovered and nurtured, but it is not made. Communal worship is experienced in ever-deepening ways when we lay aside self and serve God and others in worship.

It might be possible to have corporate worship without experiencing truly communal worship, for communal worship is the giving of ourselves to one another versus giving ourselves to the worship event. Yet the biblical ideal is that both investments are needed; both are expected. They are two dimensions in partnership with one

107

another. It is at the intersection of corporate and communal that the fullness of the blessing of worship is experienced by the grace of the Holy Spirit.

In every era God gathered persons to form communities for worship:

> God called Abram to make of him a great nation in order to bless others (Gen 12:2).

> God called Moses to assemble the nation of Israel for the purpose of covenantal worship (Gen 24:1-8).

> God called David to centralize Israel's worship in Jerusalem (1 Chr 21:29–22:1) and his son Solomon to build an extravagant temple where all God's people would gather to maintain their relationship with God and each other (1 Chr 22:6-10).

> God called out the church as an assembly in which the living presence of Jesus Christ would be found in the center of the community (Matt 18:20).

> God called all believers to identify as "a chosen race, a royal priesthood, a holy nation, a people who are God's own possession.... Once you weren't a people, but now you are God's people" (1 Pet 2:9, 10a).

> Finally, at the end of time, God will assemble a congregation in heaven "from every nation, tribe, people, and language" (Rev 7:9) so vast in number that no one can count them as they offer loud praise to God and to the Lamb.

In this chapter we explore the beautiful dynamic of worshiping in community as the body of Christ. To help us discover the deeply communal nature of worship, we turn to Jesus to discover his engagement in community as one worshiper among many.

How did Jesus participate in communal worship?

Key Question: How did Jesus participate in communal worship?

Discovering How Jesus Worshiped

Ancient Jewish culture was highly communal. Family groups, both immediate and extended, formed the central axis of life. All aspects of Jewish life were communal, and worship was no exception. Jesus was highly engaged in community both in his worship at temple and synagogue, as well as many informal occasions throughout his ministry. Jesus loved people. He was in community with those who were of his own biological and national heritage (the Israelites) and, to the dismay of many, also with Gentiles and the marginalized (the poor, lepers, noted sinners). It is no surprise, then, to discover the many occasions on which Jesus is an active participant in corporate worship, both formally and informally.

Formal Worship in Community

As we have noted in an earlier chapter, Jesus was faithful to the set times for worship in community—at temple, synagogue, and participation in holy days and festivals. Beyond mere attendance, however, Jesus was also remarkably engaged in the community of worship leaders. Jewish males shared leadership roles in the synagogue service by leading in prayer, reading the scripture lessons appointed for the day, and interpreting the scripture readings. Jesus served in all of these capacities. Several roles stand out as interesting examples of his communal involvement in worship.

Jesus served as *lector* in the synagogue. A lector is the designated reader of scripture. On one occasion, Luke describes a dramatic moment when Jesus stood to read the assigned lesson. Ironically, the passage was from Isaiah, describing Jesus's own ministry: "The Spirit of the Lord is upon me, because the Lord has anointed me. He has sent me to preach good news to the poor, to proclaim release to the prisoners and recovery of sight to the blind, to liberate the oppressed, and to proclaim the year of the Lord's favor" (Luke 4:18-19).

Jesus served as *interpreter*. It was customary for someone to explain the scripture reading by providing commentary. On this occasion, Jesus's explanation included the words "Today, this scripture has been fulfilled just as you heard it" (Luke 4:21).

Jesus *presided at the liturgy* of Passover. The sacred words and actions that accompanied the Passover meal were entrusted to the head of household or rabbi. On the night before Jesus died, he presided at the Passover meal with his disciples, offering the prayers, reading the scriptures, leading the designated psalms, serving the meal.

Jesus *led singing*. At the same Passover meal, as Jesus concluded the liturgy, Matthew notes, "Then, after singing songs of praise, they went to the Mount of Olives" (Matt 26:30; see also Mark 14:26). Have you ever thought about Jesus *singing* in worship? It's quite a thought! Yet Jesus sang in worship during his earthly ministry. Prayers and scriptures would have been chanted (sung) at synagogue and temple during Jesus's time. Jesus still sings. In Hebrews 2:12, the Incarnate Jesus declares to God, "I will praise [*hymnesō*] you [God]." It is equivalent to saying, "I will hymn you, God." The worship-leading Jesus is the singing Jesus.

Jesus *led sacramental actions*. Also on the night before Jesus died, he instituted a sacramental action[1] to be carried out among his followers: the act of washing feet. Jesus shocked his twelve disciples by stooping to wash their feet, a gesture unbefitting a person of important position such as their rabbi. Yet Jesus understood how important it was to emphasize service as the way of life among his followers. Jesus told them, "I have given you an example: Just as I have done, you also must do. I assure you, servants aren't greater than their master, nor are those who are sent greater than the one who sent them" (John 13:15-16).

From all of these examples and more, we see Jesus highly invested in formalized settings of communal worship.

Informal Worship in Community

There are also plenty of examples of informal worship settings that likewise emphasize Jesus's appreciation for community.

Jesus *pronounced blessings* upon people. He held and blessed little children (Mark 10:13-16); he blessed his eleven disciples while he ascended to the Father (Luke 24:50-51); the evening of his resurrection, Jesus blessed his disciples with peace (John 20:21, 26). "The bestowing of peace on people who acknowledge the power and presence of God is a crucial aspect of Christian worship."[2]

Jesus *gave thanks at meals*. He prayed at communal meals to give thanks for God's provision when he fed great crowds of thousands (Mark 6:41, Matt 15:36); he gave thanks for the bread and wine at Passover meals (Mark 14:22-23); he blessed the bread at a meal in the home of two disciples at Emmaus (Luke 24:30).

Jesus led in *small group prayer*. On occasion, Jesus prayed in smaller, intimate settings with his disciples. Out of one of these prayer times came the most important discussion Jesus ever had with the Twelve. He asked them, "Who do you say that I am?" Peter answered, "The Christ sent from God." It was the open door Jesus needed to explain his forthcoming suffering and the high cost of following him. (See Luke 9:18-27.) About eight days later, Jesus invited his closest disciples, Peter, John, and James, to join him up on a mountain to pray. While in prayer, Jesus's face changed and his clothing flashed like lightening. Moses and Elijah also appeared in heavenly splendor to prophesy concerning the approaching end to Jesus's earthly mission. Once again, Jesus's identity was revealed by the Father's voice from heaven: "This is my Son, my chosen one. Listen to him!" (Luke 9:35). These informal times of small group prayer became the platform for communicating the deep realities of God's eternal plan to Jesus's followers.

111

Teaching on Worship in Community

Jesus modeled deep communal involvement in worship but he went further; he explicitly instructed his disciples in the fine art of worshiping in community.

He taught them how to give as a community, giving sacrificially, not just from their surplus (Mark 12:41-44). Don't be a hypocrite by legalistically adhering to the strictest rules for giving while ignoring the more important intent of the Law—justice, peace, and faith (Matt 23:23). "You filter out an ant but swallow a camel" (Matt 23:24).

He taught them how to pray as a community. When one of Jesus's disciples asked him to train them in the art of prayer, Jesus's response was to do just that—to give them a model for the prayer of all prayers, what we now refer to as the Lord's Prayer (Luke 11:1-4), a prayer the church has prayed ever since.[3] This request came as a direct result of witnessing Jesus pray. He modeled a life of prayer, and then he instructed them in the model.

Perhaps most of all, Jesus did not want them to miss the connection between authentic relationships and authentic worship. He had a lot to say about honest relationships as a prerequisite for true worship. There is a connection between our relationship with God and being right with other people. Jesus taught his followers, "If you bring your gift to the altar and there remember that your brother or sister has something against you, leave your gift at the altar and go. First make things right with your brother or sister and then come back and offer your gift" (Matt 5:23-24). Pure relationships are valued for pure worship. Jesus places the responsibility for repairing a broken relationship with us, not the one harboring resentment against us. We are to take the first steps to be in proper fellowship so that our worship is unhindered. The shoe is also on the other foot: our forgiveness of others is crucial for God-pleasing worship. Again, Jesus instructs his disciples, "Whenever you stand up to pray, if you have something against anyone, forgive so that your Father in heaven may forgive you your wrongdoings" (Mark 11:24-25). Reconciliation is the basis of worship in community. Forgiveness is the way.

Worship in community is all about relationships. This is the theme of Jesus's prayer just before he went to the garden of Gethsemane to face his arrest. One of the last prayers to come from his lips was that believers "be made perfectly one" (John 17:23). This prayer Jesus voiced was for us, too, not just for those who formed his small band of followers in Jerusalem that night: "I'm not praying only for them but also for those who believe in me because of their word" (17:20). His prayer continues even now as he intercedes for genuine unity among his followers. (See 17:26.)

Deliberating How Jesus Would Worship Today

Weekly worship is always done in the fellowship of followers of Jesus. This fellowship has several layers to it, as we will now see. Communal worship comprises concentric circles of fellowship.

Local Fellowship. The most immediate expression of the fellowship at worship is the face-to-face, local body of believers that gathers weekly for the purpose of giving glory to God, bearing witness to our identity as God's people, proclaiming and celebrating God's story, and receiving power for living according to God's purposes. The local church gathered at an appointed time and place is the heart of communal worship.[4] This fellowship is a precious gift from God made possible by the uniting power of the Holy Spirit.

Associated Fellowship. At the same time, communal worship is not limited to local church gatherings. It's so much deeper and richer than that. A local church at worship is very often also part of a large culture of like-minded worshipers such as a denomination or movement or association.[5] Regardless of how tight or loose the organizational structure is between local church and larger church, every time the church worships, its members are aware of others in their "tribe" who share the same passion and perspective. While they are not gathered in the same location, their spirit is very much united in purpose. It is good to feel connected to folks who share the same long-standing historical and theological tradition.

Global Fellowship. An especially beautiful reality of the communal church at worship is the global church. Every Lord's Day in every time zone, there are devoted Christians worshiping the triune God. Whether under the shade of a tree, in a rice paddy, by a creek bed, or in a grand cathedral, Christ-followers all over the planet are praying and singing in indigenous ways using their heart languages. Whether openly or in hiding (some worshipers lip-synch their hymns for fear of persecution), God's got a church that encircles the globe. What a marvelous reality that God is a God of all the nations.

Wherever God's church is worshiping, it does so in simultaneous communion with sisters and brothers who are part of the Spirit-born fellowship of worshipers all over this wonderful world. The Incarnate Son collects our worship in every tongue and presents it to the Father as one voice. Help your church to rejoice in profound recognition that the family of God extends to a worldwide circle of worshipers.

Glorified Fellowship. Have you ever heard the sound of someone singing or praying and wondered where it was coming from? When we worship in community the opposite happens: we know where worship is coming from even though we can't hear the voices. All of the saints who have died before us form one huge, ongoing worshiping community in the heavenly realm. Their vocation is incessant praise—a cacophony of glorious sound. All those who have died in the Lord from the beginning of time, along with the created heavenly beings, are part of our community as well. (Or perhaps we are part of *their* community!) When we worship, we would do well to imagine that our worship is subsumed up into the eternal worship of the church triumphant. We are very much a part of the glorified[6] fellowship that stretches from earth to heaven, from now to eternity.

When we worship, we should put our 3-D glasses on. Then we can see, hear, touch, taste, and smell the great congregation that encompasses all of those who worship God together: local, associated, global, and glorified. These special layers of fellowship surround each other much like concentric circles. Starting from the center, each ring of the circle is embraced by the next layer of fellowship until the outer ring, which surrounds them all, is reached. Heavenly worship, the outer ring, is the ultimate fellowship, holding them all together.

Worshiping in community activates the horizontal dynamic of worship. The body is edified when all participants are fully engaged in offering corporate actions that stir up zeal and encourage each other to love God more deeply, serve God more devotedly, and care for each other more sincerely. (Examples of worship elements that represent horizontal direction are provided in chapter 6.) The horizontal aspect of worship is reminiscent of how the earliest believers experienced community: they "devoted themselves to the apostles' teaching, to the community, to their shared meals, and to their prayers" (Acts 2:42). The beauty of expressing human-to-human relationships can make God-to-human relationship more tangible and real.

Current Challenges

As beautiful as this sounds to us, as much as we long to experience true Christian community, occasionally we place obstacles in our own way.

† GENERATIONAL WORSHIP CHALLENGES COMMUNITY

Over the last several decades it has been popular in many churches to separate worshipers by age. Children, youth, and adults are dispersed to their own locations with the assumption that their worship is enhanced when surrounded by persons of common interests. Actually, intergenerational worship has much to offer the faith formation of *all* ages. Much of our faith is "caught" in worship more than "taught." Appreciation for the whole body of Christ is very important in worship.

Staying in our own comfort zone challenges community. It is natural to want to worship with people who are similar to us, be they of the same social status, interests, race, nationality, or political views. It can be difficult to stretch our boundaries to include people who look and act differently than we do. The church growth movement of the last half of the twentieth century actually urged churches to identify a "target group" of persons to emphasize in worship—the group that the church would focus upon above all others for the sake of ministry and numeric growth. Often this resulted in homogeneous groups. Such an approach may identify who is *in*, but it also identifies who is *out*. This can work against true community. It asks the wrong question: not "Who is my neighbor?" but "Who do I wish my neighbor was?" Worshiping in community accepts the neighbors God has given us to love; it challenges us to draw the circle bigger to encompass those who are dissimilar to us.

† COMPETING WORSHIP STYLES CHALLENGE COMMUNITY

The last fifty years have produced huge shifts in the worship landscape as churches wrestled with stylistic issues. Actually, it turned out to be less of a wrestling match and more of a worship war, as it is often referred to. Many churches decided to offer multiple services to accommodate the multiple worship style preferences of their people. The upside: our appreciation for new ways to worship has expanded. The downside: congregations became segregated into preference groups. I continue to regularly hear from leaders across the country who bemoan the fact that stylistically driven venues have resulted in a divided church. In time, other congregations made the decision to drive their stake in the sand and go entirely in one direction or the other, letting other churches minister to people of other preference groups.

Thankfully, many churches are rethinking the wisdom of either of these approaches. Leaders are beginning to pursue the important work of how to become one church again by addressing more significant issues of community, rather than merely trying to keep up with worship trends. Worshiping in community can be hindered by an overestimation of the value of cosmetic worship styles (of any kind). Ultimately it is about relationships, not styles.

† INTERNET WORSHIP CHALLENGES COMMUNITY

Many churches today broadcast their worship services via the Internet. This form of access to local church services has many advantages. For church members, it is especially helpful to those who are prevented from attending due to illness, are away on business, or are on vacation. It's a great way to stay in touch with God and others. For other people who are more permanently prevented from coming to church (for example, prisoners, college students away from home, missionaries), and for the Internet surfers who stumble upon your site, your service can be a real source of inspiration and hope.

At the same time, Internet worship services may weaken community when they are consistently used for convenience, or as an excuse to not engage in person with fellow believers. People can hide behind a computer screen because it requires much less of them. When this happens, the service can become "simulation worship," a virtual reality, not the real thing. That's not to say these persons do not benefit from the service (they likely do); but neither are they *contributing* to the fellowship of believers, which is, as we have found, absolutely vital to biblical worship. It can even lead to an increased sense of isolation. Internet services must not substitute for the

117

person-to-person interaction that encourages the worship of one's local church.

There will always be things that can challenge the regular, ongoing meeting of a local body of Christian disciples with the triune God who are gathered to express acts of corporate devotion in partnership with one another. Whenever possible we must contend for each member participating in person for the good of the whole.

HWJW?

How would Jesus worship if he were here among us today? He would enter in as a full participant within a local fellowship of worshipers. He would take up his formal leadership roles in the community. He would engage in informal occasions for worship. In short, he would invest totally in worship, as one of the community but also for the sake of the community, contributing to the rich experience of all. Do you hear the call—the call of Jesus? "Come follow me...by participating fully in the community of worshipers where God has placed you."

HWJW? He would enter in as a full participant with a local fellowship of worshipers.

Determining How I Will Worship

Reflection

After looking at Jesus, our role model for worship, it's time to determine what adjustments our Master Teacher may be asking of his disciples. To begin, consider these questions:

- Which best describes your church's worship: corporate, communal, or both? Explain.

- Do you believe you personally participate in worship more independently or interdependently? Explain.

- Choose one of the ways that Jesus instructed his disciples about being a participant in worship: how to give, how to pray, how to reconcile/forgive others. Which one speaks to you the most? Why?

- "Worship in community is all about relationships." If you were to hear Jesus say this today, put into your own words what he might mean.

- Of the four circles of fellowship (local, associated, global, glorified), which would you like to explore further? Why? How might you begin?

- Of the four current challenges mentioned in this chapter, which one might your community benefit from discussing further?

Imagine

It's next Sunday. You head to church with a new appreciation for all of the people that will gather there. You give God thanks for the gift of each person. You catch yourself smiling as you think of the children who will worship with you. You pray for all Christians who are gathering this Lord's Day to worship God throughout the world. You imagine how differently each worship space looks, marveling at how vast the kingdom of God is.

- Identify one specific way that you could deepen the fellowship of believers in your church by contributing to the worship of others.

- What one concrete action step will you take to appreciate one of the circles of fellowship of which you tend to be less aware?

Action

With God's help, I determine to participate more fully in the fellowship of believers at worship by _____. (Be specific.)

Prayer

Our Father, who art in heaven,
Hallowed be thy Name.
Thy Kingdom come,
thy will be done on earth,
as it is in heaven.
Give us this day our daily bread.
And forgive us our trespasses,
as we forgive those that trespass against us.
And lead us not into temptation,
but deliver us from evil.
For thine is the kingdom,
and the power,
and the glory, forever.
Amen.

THE SENDING FROM
WORSHIP

This book began with the call to worship like Jesus. He is the guide and we are his followers. Each chapter ended with the same invitation: Do you hear the call of Jesus? "Come, follow me in worship." But there is one more way that Jesus leads us in worship, and that is out into the world as we are sent from worship. In worship we receive power for living according to God's kingdom purposes.

Jesus connects love of God in corporate worship with love of neighbor 24-7. His commitment to the first commandment, loving God with all one's heart, soul, mind, and strength, overflowed into his commitment to the second commandment, which "is equally important: 'Love your neighbor as yourself.' No other commandment is greater than these" (Mark 12:31 NLT). Loving God and loving others is the living out of the whole of the Great Commandment. Loving God is more than keeping the Sabbath and shunning idol worship. Loving God includes loving others too—all others.

Love for God leads to love for people. Surely that is what the Apostle John was recalling from his own days of following Jesus when he wrote, "This commandment we have from him: Those who claim to love God ought to love their brother and sister also" (1 John 4:21).

We must not, however, make the mistake that loving God and loving neighbor are the same thing. Each one is distinct in its purpose and character. While related, they are not the same. Neither must we substitute one for the other. Our discipleship is imperfect without the union of Lord's Day worship *and* doing justice, loving mercy, and walking humbly with our God. (See Micah 6:1-8, where all three are emphasized.) When we love God entirely, with every aspect of our being, we are changed forever into the likeness of Jesus and able to love people. John Wesley referred to this as Perfect Love.[1]

One of the great challenges of modern Christianity is the misunderstanding of the relationship between worship and our daily lives. Frankly, it has sometimes led to the church's weakened witness: "The divorce of liturgy and living, of prayer and practice, is more than a scandal; it is a disaster."[2]

However, there is good news! Jesus has gone before us to show us the way. We follow our guide out into the world, but we don't just follow, we are sent. We are sent from worship inspired and empowered by the Holy Spirit to continue our worship in our daily lives. Christian worship becomes an uninterrupted continuum of blessing to God and blessing to others. When this happens, we will know what it means to truly worship like Jesus.

NOTES

1. Our Role Model for Worship

1. See Deut 4:9-10, 39-40; 6:5-9; Ps 78:1-8

2. Pasquato Ottorino, "Catechesis—Discipleship," in *Encyclopedia of Ancient Christianity*, ed. Thomas C. Oden and Joel C. Elowsky (Downers Grove, IL: InterVarsity, 2014), 1:458.

3. Pronounced kat-e-*kee*-sis.

4. Pasquato Ottorino, "Catechesis," in Oden and Elowsky, *Encyclopedia of Ancient Christianity*, 1:443.

5 Pasquato Ottorino, "Catechesis," in Oden and Elowsky, *Encyclopedia of Ancient Christianity*, 1:443.

6. Pasquato Ottorino, "Catechumenate—Discipleship," in Oden and Elowsky, *Encyclopedia of Ancient Christianity*, 1:458.

2. The Priority of Worship

1. Different Protestant denominations refer to baptism and Holy Communion by one of these two terms.

2. The Christian God is One God in Three Persons: Father, Son, and Holy Spirit (triune). (See chapter 4 in this book.)

3. Jesus in human flesh.

4. Sean A. Harrison, "Jesus' Prayers," in *NLT Illustrated Study Bible* (Carol Stream, IL: Tyndale), 1,855.

5. Harold M. Best, *Unceasing Worship: Biblical Perspectives on Worship and the Arts* (Downers Grove, IL: InterVarsity, 2003), 24–25.

6. Attributed to Karl Barth.

7. *Outreach* magazine, "7 Startling Facts: An Up Close Look at Church Attendance in America," Church Leaders, April 10, 2018, accessed June 4, 2018, https://churchleaders.com/pastors/pastor-articles/139575-7-startling-facts-an-up-close-look-at-church-attendance-in-america.html.

8. *Outreach* Magazine, "7 Startling Facts."

9. *Outreach* Magazine, "7 Startling Facts."

10. *Outreach* Magazine, "7 Startling Facts."

11. Barna Group, "The State of the Church 2016," *State of the Church & Family Report*, September 16, 2016, accessed June 4, 2018, https://www.barna.com/research/state-church-2016/.

12. Barna Group.

13. Gallup former editor in chief Frank Newport agrees that surveys are affected by the fact that many people tend to present themselves somewhat optimistically. (See *Outreach* magazine, "7 Startling Facts.")

14. See "Attendance at Religious Services," Pew Research Center, accessed January 2019, http://www.pewforum.org/religious-landscape-study/attendance-at-religious-services/.

15. Franklin M. Segler, *Understanding, Preparing for, and Practicing Christian Worship* (revised by Randall Brandley), 2nd ed. (Nashville: Broadman and Holman, 1996), 10–11.

16. A. W. Tozer, *A Disruptive Faith: Expect God to Interrupt Your Life*, ed. James L. Snyder (Ventura, CA: Regal, 2011), 5.

3. The Object of Worship

1. See Gen 3:4-5 (also Rom 1:25) and Rev 19:20.

2. One or more of these terms may be used to refer to the true God, but not without clarification. That is the point; the terms are vague enough to be unclear as to exactly who is being worshiped. Recently a student chose a song for a worship assignment that referred only to a vague term for God. I typed the phrase from the song on an Internet search engine. The first hit was "pagan songs." It was actually published by one of the largest modern worship music producers in

the world. While her intention was certainly not to mislead any worshipers, she could inadvertently have done so.

3. C. K. Barrett, noted Johannine scholar, held this view. See C. K. Barrett, *The Gospel According to St. John: An Introduction with Commentary and Notes on the Greek Text* (Philadelphia: Westminster, 1978), 283.

4. Marianne Meye Thompson, "Worshiping in Spirit and in Truth" (plenary address, Calvin Symposium on Worship, Grand Rapids, MI, January 26, 2018).

5. *United States Catholic Catechism for Adults* (Washington, DC: United States Conference of Catholic Bishops, 2006), 51.

6. Sean A. Harrison, study notes on Matthew 6:9, in *NLT Illustrated Study Bible* (Carol Stream, IL: Tyndale, 2015), 1,689. Italics original.

7. Robert E. Webber, *Worship Is a Verb: Celebrating God's Mighty Deeds of Salvation* (Peabody, MA: Hendrickson, 1996), 66. Italics original.

8. A. W. Tozer, *Man: The Dwelling Place of God* (Harrisburg, PA: Christian Publications, 1966), 136.

9. A. W. Tozer, *The Knowledge of the Holy* (Harrisburg, PA: Christian Publications, 2012), 9.

4. The Central Figure of Worship

1. The Incarnation is the reality that Jesus, who is the eternal Word of God, was given flesh to live as a human within the created order—the very order that he co-created. *Carne* is Latin for "flesh." The One who previously had no flesh was given a human body.

2. John Russell, "Deliberate" (essay, Robert E. Webber Institute for Worship Studies, 2018), 3.

3. Larry W. Hurtado, *At the Origins of Christian Worship: The Context and Character of Earliest Christian Devotion* (Grand Rapids: Eerdmans, 1999), 74–92. (These and many examples of early Christian Christ-devotion are elaborated upon in detail.)

4. See the Nicene Creed.

5. The relationship of the Persons of the Trinity has been depicted as a dance (*perichoresis*) by the church fathers.

6. Bryan Chapell, *Christ-Centered Worship: Letting the Gospel Shape Our Practice* (Grand Rapids: Baker Academic, 2009), 112–13.

7. James B. Torrance, *Worship, Community and the Triune God of Grace* (Downers Grove, IL: InterVarsity, 1996), 14–15.

8. C. S. Lewis, *The Screwtape Letters* (New York: HarperCollins, 1996), excerpts from 135–39. Italics original.

9. Each of these examples is documented.

10. John Jefferson Davis, *Worship and the Reality of God: An Evangelical Theology of Real Presence* (Downers Grove, IL: InterVarsity, 2010), 17. Italics original.

11. Dorothy L. Sayers, *Letters to a Diminished Church: Passionate Arguments for the Relevance of Christian Doctrine* (Nashville: W Publishing Group, 2004), 20–21.

5. The Divine Narrative of Worship

1. James K. A. Smith, *You Are What You Love: The Spiritual Power of Habit* (Grand Rapids, MI: Brazos, 2016), 46.

2. Smith, *You Are What You Love*, 47.

3. Robert E. Webber, *Ancient-Future Worship: Proclaiming and Enacting God's Narrative* (Grand Rapids: Baker, 2008), 43.

4. Yunusa Nmadu, quoted in Jeremy Weber, "No Cheeks Left to Turn: The Double Persecution of Africa's Largest Church," *Christianity Today* 62, no. 9 (November 2018): 32.

5. Justo L. González, *A Brief History of Sunday: From the New Testament to the New Creation* (Grand Rapids: Eerdmans, 2017), 5.

6. Creation establishes the seven-day cycle, Incarnation celebrates the day of Christ's Resurrection, Re-Creation is anticipated as eternal worship. The Lord's Day encompasses it all.

7. Robert E. Webber, *Who Gets to Narrate the World? Contending for the Christian Story in an Age of Rivals* (Downers Grove, IL: InterVarsity, 2008), 11. Italics original.

8. Webber, *Ancient-Future Worship*, 40.

9. Robert E. Webber, *The Divine Embrace: Recovering the Passionate Spiritual Life* (Grand Rapids: Baker, 2006), 231.

10. Webber, *Ancient-Future Worship*, 23.

11. Richard John Neuhaus, *Freedom for Ministry* (San Francisco: Harper and Row, 1979), 127.

12. Webber, *Ancient-Future Worship*, 43.

6. The Conversation of Worship

1. Marianne Meye Thompson, "Worshiping in Spirit and in Truth" (plenary address, Calvin Symposium on Worship, Grand Rapids, January 26, 2018).

2. Thompson, "Worshiping in Spirit and in Truth."

3. Thompson, "Worshiping in Spirit and in Truth."

4. Gerald L. Borchert, *The New American Commentary: An Exegetical and Theological Exposition of Holy Scripture* (New International Version), vol. 25A (Nashville: Broadman and Holman, 1996), 208.

5. After the Reformation in the sixteenth century, many Protestants ceased to celebrate weekly Communion (and still do not). However, some thoughtfully planned response to the word is always needed for biblical worship.

7. The Disciple as Participant of Worship

1. See Exod 13:2 and Lev 12:8.

2. The word *shema* is taken from the first word of Deut 6:4 in Hebrew: *sh'ma* means "hear." (*Hear*, O Israel...)

3. The Great Commandment also included loving one's neighbor as oneself (Mark 12:29-31). Though sometimes referred to as two commandments, they actually form one commandment as seen in verse 31.

4. Jesus adds "mind" to the wording of the *Shema*.

5. Francis Foulkes, "Synagogue," in *Baker Encyclopedia of the*

Bible, ed. Walter A. Elwell, vol. 4, (Grand Rapids: Baker, 1988), 2008.

6. Daniel I. Block, *For the Glory of God: Recovering a Biblical Theology of Worship* (Grand Rapids: Baker Academic, 2014), 102.

7. Simon Chan, *Liturgical Theology: The Church as Worshiping Community* (Downers Grove, IL: InterVarsity Academic, 2006), 15. Italics original.

8. William Harmless, SJ, ed., *Augustine in His Own Words* (Washington, DC: Catholic University of America Press, 2010), 147.

9. Robert E. Webber, *Journey to Jesus: The Worship, Evangelism, and Nurture Mission of the Church* (Nashville: Abingdon, 2001), 84.

10. Webber, *Journey to Jesus*, 85.

11. Chan, *Liturgical Theology*, 53. Italics original.

12. Harold M. Best, *Unceasing Worship: Biblical Perspectives on Worship and the Arts* (Downers Grove, IL: InterVarsity, 2003), 77.

8. The Community of Worship

1. The washing of feet is not normally viewed as an official sacrament of the church, but it is sacramental in nature simply because it affords the opportunity to encounter Christ and be changed.

2. Gerald L. Borchert, *Worship in the New Testament: Divine Mystery and Human Response* (Saint Louis: Chalice, 2008), 36.

3. Believers in the early church prayed the Lord's Prayer three times daily as an adaptation of the Jewish custom of prayer hours.

4. Remember, the church is not a building but a people. People who assemble as the church do so in many different settings.

5. There are truly independent churches that exist, of course. However, the majority of churches in North America have some relationship with other churches with whom they identify.

6. "Glorified bodies" refers to resurrected bodies—the new, heavenly bodies we will inherit that will never experience death, decay, illness, or the consequences of sin.

The Sending from Worship

1. John Wesley, "Christian Perfection," *The Works of John Wesley*, ed. Thomas Jackson (London: Wesleyan Methodist Book Room, 1872; reprint by Baker Book House, 1978), VI: 413; John Telford, ed., *The Letters of John Wesley, A.M.* (London: Epworth, 1931), 4:187; 7:120.

2. Abraham Joshua Heschel, *Moral Grandeur and Spiritual Audacity*, ed. Susannah Heschel (New York: Farrar, Straus and Giroux, 1997), 261.

Made in the USA
Columbia, SC
07 September 2021

44992483R00080